Veidre Thomas
18461 Crownhill Dr
South Bend IN 46637

W9-ARW-146

ESSENTIAL
SUFISM

ESSENTIAL

SUFISM

EDITED BY
James Fadiman and Robert Frager

CASTLE BOOKS

SUFISM

Library of Congress Cataloging-in-Publication Data
Essential sufism / edited by James Fadiman and Robert Frager.
San Francisco : HarperSanFrancisco, 1997.

Published by CASTLE BOOKS
A Division of Book Sales, Inc.
114 Northfield Avenue, Edison, New Jersey 08837

ISBN 0-7858-0906-6

Acknowledgments

We'd like to thank Coleman Barks for his support, Tom Grady and Laura Harger for their initial editorial enthusiasm, and John Louden, Karen Levine, Terri Leonard, Carl Walesa, and Martha Blegen for thier final editorial and design inputs. Special thanks to Jeanette Berson for her ideas and help at numerous critical junctions.

We couldn't have attempted or completed this book without the guidance of our own teaches and the suggestions and generosity of many Sufi students, teachers, and publishers.

Contents

Foreword ⌣ *Huston Smith*   IX

Introduction ⌣ *Sheikh Ragip Robert Frager al Jerrahi*   1

PART ONE
The Many Faces of Sufism
   CHAPTER 1: The Sufi Way   35

PART TWO
Living in the World
   CHAPTER 2: Daily Life   45
   CHAPTER 3: Self-Deception and Self-Knowledge   57
   CHAPTER 4: The Lower Self   65
   CHAPTER 5: The World, Mirror of the Divine   73
   CHAPTER 6: Wisdom   79
   CHAPTER 7: Hadith, the Words of the Prophet   87

PART THREE
Love and an Open Heart
   CHAPTER 8: Spiritual Experience   95
   CHAPTER 9: Opening the Heart   101
   CHAPTER 10: Contemplation and Knowledge   107
   CHAPTER 11: Love   113

PART FOUR
Sufi Teachers
    CHAPTER 12: Teachers and Students   127

PART FIVE
Sufism in Action
    CHAPTER 13: Practices   151
    CHAPTER 14: Sufi Humor   161
    CHAPTER 15: Virtues   171
        Faith   171
        Humility   174
        Gratitude   178
        Poverty   180
        Patience   183
        Generosity   185

PART SIX
In Touch with the Divine
    CHAPTER 16: How to Know God   197
    CHAPTER 17: Prayer   203
    CHAPTER 18: Remembrance of God   209
    CHAPTER 19: Service   217

PART SEVEN
Faces of the One
    CHAPTER 20: God   227
    CHAPTER 21: Satan   235

PART EIGHT
Transformation
    CHAPTER 22: Self-Transformation   243
    CHAPTER 23: Death   251

    A Note on the Texts and Calligraphy   257
    Bibliography   259
    Permission Acknowledgments   263

The Sufis are the mystics of Islam. Every upright Muslim expects to see God after death, but the Sufis are the impatient ones. They want God now—moment by moment, day by day, in this very life. And they are willing to undergo the disciplines that make that possible. This book presents selections from a multitude of saints and sages whose hearts were opened through the Sufi path. One of the greatest of them, Jalal-ad-Din al-Rumi, pointed out that "there are hundreds of ways to kiss the ground." This book shows us some of them.

Three modes of union with the divine turn up in every religious tradition and all three are present in Sufism. One of these is ecstatic. It requires a special visitation that lifts the soul out of its body—*ex* (out), *statuo* (to stand), *ecstasis* (to stand outside oneself)—and transports it to a higher, distinctly different level of consciousness that relativizes our normal register dramatically. The experience can be so intense that it sends the body into convulsions.

Sufis honor their ecstatics, but they refer to them (affectionately) as "spiritual drunkards" because their God-intoxication dissociates them from the ordinary world. A famous account—whether it is fact or legend the Sufis do not say—tells of a youth who stepped into his garden one morning, heard a bird sing, and was transported. When he regained his normal consciousness, forty years had elapsed.

Sufis, as I say, honor their ecstatics; but then their practical streak—reminiscent of Zen Buddhism—takes over and leads them to position a second category of mystics above them. We could call them Gnostic Sufis (from the Greek word for knowledge, *gnosis*), but that word has acquired connotations that could mislead us, so intellective Sufis—from *intellectus,* the Latin counterpart of *gnosi*—serves better. (The Arabic equivalent of these words, *ma'rifah,* is unsuitable because it has no English derivative.) Like the jnana yogis of Hinduism, intellective Sufis find God by knowing him, but their mode of knowing is intuitive rather than factual. Eunice Tietjens puts her finger on that mode in her poem in *Everest: The West Ridge,* which I quote with emphasis added.

> The stone grows old.
> Eternity is not for stones.
> But I shall go down from this airy space, this swift
>   white peace, this stinging exultation;
> And time will close about me, and my soul stir to the rhythm
>   of the daily round.
> Yet, *having known,* life will not press so close.
> And always I shall feel time ravel thin about me.
> For once I stood
> in the white windy presence of eternity.

Because the object of the religious life is not altered states but altered traits of character—Arthur Deikman pointed this out in the psychedelic sixties, but was insufficiently listened to—Sufis consider ecstatic God-consciousness incomplete until it has been brought back and integrated with daily life. Because intellective Sufis effect this integration, Muslims see them as "sober." They are the counterparts of Plato's philosopher who, once he has seen the sun, returns to the cave with his new-found understanding of what shadows actually are. Some of them relativize even Plato's sun. "Wist thou not that the sun thou seest is but a reflection of the Sun behind the veil?"

The third class of Sufis is the largest because it taps into what may be the strongest emotion in the human heart, though much in society represses it. That emotion is love, and Sufi love poetry is world famous. A year or two ago, its all-time master (the Rumi I have already mentioned) was the best-selling poet in America. Rabi'a was not as prolific, but in quality she was Rumi's equal, as the following excerpt testifies.

My God and my Lord:

Eyes are at rest, the stars are setting. Hushed are the movements of birds in their nests, of monsters in the sea; and You are the Just Who knows no change; the Equity that does not swerve, the everlasting that never passes away. The doors of kings are locked now and guarded by their henchmen, but your door is open to all who call upon You. My Lord, each lover is now alone with his beloved. And I am alone with Thee.

It is to the lovers in Sufism that this book opens its pages. In what often seems like a loveless age—ours, but was it ever different?—James Fadiman and Robert Frager deserve our thanks for giving them this added hearing.

Huston Smith
Berkeley, California

Introduction

SHEIKH RAGIP ROBERT FRAGER AL JERRAHI

Know, O beloved, that man was not created in jest
or at random, but marvelously made
and for some great end.

AL-GHAZZALI

For thousands of years, Sufism has offered a path on which one can progress toward the "great end" of Self-realization, or God-realization. Sufism is a way of love, a way of devotion, and a way of knowledge.

There is no single, systematic approach to Sufi teachings, and not all of its teachings can be communicated in words. The wisdom of Sufism can be found in stories, poetry, art, calligraphy, rituals, exercises, readings, dance movements, and prayer.

Sufism is often described as a path, suggesting both an origin and a destination. The aim of Sufism is the elimination of all veils between the individual and God. Traveling this path, one can acquire knowledge of Reality. God is the ultimate reality, not this phenomenal world of multiplicity.

To understand Sufism, we must understand mysticism. The Greek root *myein*, "to close the eyes," is also the root of "mystery"; the mystic's goal is not to be reached by the intellect or by ordinary means. Fundamentally, mysticism is love of the Absolute, the One Reality, also called Truth, Love, or God. According to Sarraj's classic definition of Sufism, "The Sufis are people who prefer God to everything and God prefers them to everything else."

For the Sufis, not only love but also self-knowledge leads to knowledge of God. The Sufi philosopher Al-Ghazzali says, "Real self-knowledge consists in knowing the following things: What are you in yourself and where did you come from? Where are you going and for what purpose are you tarrying here awhile? In what does your real happiness and misery consist?" Many pitfalls, both real and imagined, render us unable or even unwilling to seek this inner knowledge.

⌒

Historians usually describe Sufism as the mystical core of Islam and date its appearance to the beginnings of Islam, at about the ninth century A.D. According to many Sufis, however, the essential Truths of Sufism exist in all religions. The foundation for all mysticism includes the outer forms of religious practice, as well as a life based on moral and ethical principles. The roots of the tree of religion are founded in religious practices and principles, which focus on outer behavior. The branches of the tree are mysticism, the spiritual disciplines that extend the individual upward, toward the Infinite. The fruit of the tree is the Truth, or God.

In this universal sense, Sufism existed before Islam. Before the time of Muhammad, religious law had died out in Arabia and the people had lost their understanding of ethics and morality. Without the outer practice of religious law and moral principles, there could be no inner practice of Sufism. The adoption of the moral and ethical teachings of Islam created a climate in which Sufism could develop and flourish. Sufism is not different from the mysticism at the heart of all religions. Just as a river that passes through many countries and is claimed by each as its own is still only one river, all mysticism has the same goal: the direct experience of the Divine.

One who practices Sufism is called a Sufi, or dervish, or faquir. *Sufi* has several meanings in Arabic, including "pure" and "wool."

(Early Sufis wore simple wool cloaks in addition to seeking inner purity.) *Dervish* is a Persian term derived from *dar,* or "door." It refers to one who goes from door to door. (Many dervishes used to go from house to house, begging for food or lodging.) It also means one who is at the threshold (between awareness of this world and awareness of the Divine). *Faqir* is Arabic for a poor person. In Sufism this does not refer to those poor in worldly goods, but to those who are "spiritually poor," that is, those whose hearts are empty of attachment to anything other than God. They realize that they have nothing, that they can do nothing, that they are nothing without God. They rely on nothing in this world, only on God.

Sufism is most prominent in the Middle East and in Islamic countries, but its ideas, practices, and teachers are to be found throughout the world. Sufis are scattered among all nations of the world, and, like any genuine mystical tradition, Sufism has become associated with a variety of outward forms to fit the cultures and societies in which it has been practiced. Sufi groups have existed for centuries in the Middle East, North Africa, Europe, Central Asia, India, Pakistan, Indonesia, and China. In some countries Sufism is well known and widely accepted. In others, Sufism is considered heretical or even subversive because of its frequent preference for the spirit of the law over the letter.

THE FOUNDATIONS OF SUFISM

Islam, the Arabic word for "submission to God's will," is the religious tradition taught by the prophet Muhammad. The goal of Islam is to be in harmony with God, to attune the individual's will to God's will. The initial revelation of the Koran (or Qur'an) occurred in the year A.D. 610. The Islamic era dates from A.D. 622, the year Muhammad fled from Mecca to the city of Medina, persecuted by the city's leaders, who opposed the monotheistic and democratic teachings of Islam.

Islam is described in the Koran as a continuation of the great monotheistic tradition revealed in constant succession to such prophets as Abraham, Moses, and Jesus. According to one of the sayings of the prophet Muhammad, "I have not brought you a new religion. I have brought you *the* religion, in an unchanged, untampered with way."

Islam stresses honesty, charity, service, and other virtues that form a solid foundation for the spiritual practices of Sufism. A moral, ethical, and disciplined life-style is like a solid container that can hold the Sufi's mystical experience without its leaking or dissipating. In the words of my first Sufi teacher, Muzaffer Ozak, "Sufism without Islam is like a candle burning in the open without a lantern. There are winds which may blow that candle out. But if you have a lantern with glass protecting the flame, the candle will continue to burn safely."

Most Sufis believe that the great religions and mystical traditions of the world share the same essential Truth. The various prophets and spiritual teachers are like the light bulbs that illuminate a room. The bulbs are different, but the current comes from one source, which is God. It is the same light; each of the individual bulbs receives electricity from a single source. The quality of the light is always basically the same, and so is the original source.

Because all the great prophets have received their inspiration from the same Source and brought the same light, the same basic truths, to humanity, the Sufis believe that to deny even one of the prophets is to deny their universal message and common Source. When bulbs are arranged in series so that electricity passes through one bulb to get to the next, if one bulb goes out, all the lights go out.

Sufism proposes that all the great religious and spiritual teachers were sent by one God. They were all true teachers, and what they taught was true. Their teachings originated from the same Divine Source. There is no fundamental difference among all the spiritual teachers and what they have brought; however, just as some bulbs give more light, some teachers have illuminated more of humanity than others. The Sufis love and accept them all, because the Sufis believe there is one God and one message and many prophets. The differences among religions are of human origin, but the truth of all religions is the same and comes from God.

The saints are those men and women who interpret the teachings of religion and live by the truth of their religion. The writings and poetry in this book are from some of the great Sufi saints. Though it may be very difficult to recognize who is a saint, one of the signs is that a saint inspires and increases the seeker's devotion to God.

The principal characteristic of the saints is that they are loved by God and they love only God. Also, because of their proximity to God, when saints pray for something, it often happens. Many saints are hidden. That is, their outer lives do not look any different from the lives of their neighbors, although their inner lives are radiant with the Divine Presence. It is said that God hides the saints and lovers of God so that people will think that everyone else might be a saint and will therefore love and care for one another.

The writings of the saints may inspire you deeply, but to become a mystic, you have to go to a mystical school. In Sufism, this generally means to study with a teacher and a group of Sufi seekers who follow in the traditions of one of the Sufi orders. Sufi groups generally meet several times a week for prayer, meditation, Sufi discourses, and other spiritual practices. You cannot teach yourself Sufism or develop spiritually by yourself any more than you can become a doctor or an engineer by yourself.

THE CREED OF FAITH

The Islamic creed of faith includes the fundamental beliefs that are basic tenets of Sufism:

I believe in God,
And in God's angels,
And in the Holy Books,
And in God's Messengers,
And in the Day of Resurrection,
And in destiny,

That all good and bad come from God,
And that there is life after this life.

1. The first article of faith is to believe that there is one God and that God is transcendent of all creation. God is before the before and after the after. God is all-powerful and needs nothing from anyone or anything. God is the owner of everything: everything that you can see and everything that you cannot see.

Sufis maintain that you don't look for God in Mecca or Jerusalem but in your heart. The paradox with which Sufis struggle is that God is very close, but humanity is far from God. Faith brings the seeker closer.

2. God's angels are instruments of Divine will. They form a series of ever more luminous beings, a hierarchy between humanity and God. This hierarchy can be viewed as an inward or an outward reality, or as both at once.

One of the sayings of the Prophet analyzes the differences between human and angelic natures: "God created the angels from intellect without sensuality, the beasts from sensuality without intellect, and humanity from both intellect and sensuality. So when a person's intellect overcomes his sensuality, he is better than the angels, but when his sensuality overcomes his intellect, he is worse than the beasts."

3. The Sufis believe in four great Books: the Torah brought by Moses, the Psalms of David, the Gospels inspired by Jesus, and the Koran revealed to Muhammad. The Sufis also believe that in addition to these scriptures, there have been hundreds of shorter scrolls revealed to other prophets.

4. Each prophet brought the same truth from the same Divine source, and therefore we have to believe in all of them. Those prophets who have brought a Book are known as Messengers.

5. God has sent humanity here to earth to learn, and when the Day of Resurrection comes, God will examine everyone's life. God

will then calculate the balance of good and bad that each person has carried out in this world.

6. The Sufis believe in fate or destiny, that nothing happens without God's will. Human will exists within the context of the greater Divine will.

7. Because the Sufis believe in God's will, they believe that all things that come to us, good and bad, pleasant and unpleasant, come from God.

8. Life does not end with death. Life in this world is like a dream, and our true life starts in the next world.

There are hundreds of millions of people who would agree with these beliefs. They believe what the Sufis believe, but they are not aware that, in spirit, they are in agreement with Sufism and Islam.

THE FIVE PILLARS OF ISLAM

For those who wish to follow Islam, there are five basic practices and many formal observances. The five pillars of Islam are bearing witness, daily prayer, fasting during the month of Ramadan, charity, and pilgrimage to Mecca.

Bearing Witness, or the Confession of Faith. Entrance into Islam begins with the recitation of these basic tenets of Islamic faith: "I bear witness that there is no god but God, and I bear witness that Muhammad is a servant and a Messenger of God."

To witness, we must be awake, conscious. To realize the truth of the assertion "There is no god but God" is to know firsthand the unity of God. To come to this realization is, in one sense, the pinnacle of the Islamic mystical path.

Daily Prayer. Five times a day there is a call to prayer; at dawn, noon, midafternoon, dusk, and night. The prayers interrupt daily activities in order to reorient members of the community to religious awareness.

Communal prayers are visible manifestations of the doctrine that all are equal in the eyes of God, irrespective of class, social, and economic distinctions. All who come to the mosque pray together, without regard to wealth or status.

Everything has both outer form and inner meaning. This is especially true in prayer. The beginning of the formal Islamic prayer is called the *tekbir*. Facing Mecca, Muslims put their hands up to their ears, palms forward, and say, *"Allah hu Ekber,"* "God is Greater." God is greater than anything and everything that God has created. As they raise their hands, they then try to put the world and any worldly concerns behind them. It is as if the world is pushed back with the backs of the hands. They then open their hearts so that they can feel that they are truly in the presence of God, with nothing separating them from God. This is the essence of prayer, a constantly held goal. It may not be possible to put aside completely all the love and care and temptations of the world, but one can try.

Fasting. Each year all Muslims who are able to do so fast from dawn to sunset for the month of Ramadan. During the fast, they are supposed to abstain from eating, drinking, smoking, and making love. It is a difficult practice, intended to help Muslims remain aware of the conflicting forces of their lower and higher natures. Al-Ghazzali describes the outer and the inner mystical levels of fasting as follows:

> The fasting of the general public involves refraining from satisfying the appetite of the stomach and the appetite of the sex. . . .
>
> The fasting of the select few is to keep the ears, the eyes, the tongue, the hands, and the feet as well as the other senses free from sin.
>
> The fasting of the elite among the select few is the fast of the heart from mean thoughts and worldly worries and its complete unconcern with anything other than God and the last day, as well as concern over this world.

Charity. Each year, at the end of the month of Ramadan, every household is asked to give one fortieth, or two and a half percent, of its accumulated wealth to the poor. It is said that all things originate from God; having goods and money is seen as custodianship, in that one retains the right to possessions by returning some of one's goods to the larger Muslim community from which they came.

Pilgrimage to Mecca. The Kaaba, the shrine in the heart of the city of Mecca in Saudi Arabia, is the most holy site in Islam. It is a stone cube said to have been built by the prophets Abraham and Ishmael. All Muslims are required to make a pilgrimage to Mecca once in their lifetime, provided they can afford to do so. There are a set of rigorous observances to be followed at the time of pilgrimage, which occurs during a specified week each year. The pilgrimage is a time in adult life when devotion to the spiritual completely overshadows our worldly interests. This annual ritual has kept the different Muslim peoples aware of their common bond.

SUFISM AND ISLAM

One of the most common questions asked of Sufi teachers is whether one can become a dervish without becoming a Muslim. According to some authorities, the answer is yes: the universal truths taught in Sufism can be practiced by any sincere seeker. According to many other authorities, the answer is no: if you are not a Muslim, you cannot become a dervish. For them, the practices of Sufism are rooted in the observances and rituals of Islam. However, not all of those who say they are Muslims can become dervishes. They have to be sincere in their faith and their belief.

According to Sheikh Safer, the head sheikh of the Halveti-Jerrahi Order, the external forms of Islam are only the beginning. There is an outer form of prayer and an inner prayer, for example. You can do the outer form for fifty years, but prayer is not just this form. You have to develop a heart that can pray as well. Finally, as the dervish evolves, there is the level of continuous inner prayer, not only five times a day. This is the ultimate goal of Sufi practice. First, you must be sincere.

There are three great blessings given to those who love God. They are *islam* (submission), *iman* (faith), and *ihsan* (awareness of

God). These are three signs of progress on the spiritual path. Islam is the complete surrender of the individual to God's will and total acceptance of the teachings of the Koran. *Iman* is the inner aspect of Islam. *Ihsan* means "to act beautifully." It is generally explained as "to worship God as if you see Him." The person who fully develops *ihsan* is aware of God at all times and has reached the goal of Sufism. This state is possible through Sufism, that is, through carrying out spiritual practice and discipline. The dervish has to work hard and with sincerity.

If God wills, these efforts will bear fruit. This is true both spiritually and materially. Many people work diligently, but not everyone who works becomes a millionaire. But some do, if God wills. By the same token, some people do become successful on the spiritual path and reach the level of constant awareness of God. The end result is in the hands of God. Some people reach this final spiritual state in forty days, others in forty years. And for some, a whole lifetime of effort is not enough. The best path is to let go and surrender to God's will.

MUHAMMAD

Muhammad (or Mohammed, A.D. 570–632) transmitted the message of the Koran to humanity. Muslims believe that he was not divine but was divinely inspired. He is looked upon in Islam as the man who comes as close as one can to living the ideal life set forth in the Koran. For the Sufis, Muhammad is a role model to be studied and imitated.

As the leader of the early Islamic community, Muhammad was very much involved with worldly as well as spiritual issues. He successfully settled political disputes, led armies, married, and raised children, in addition to instructing his followers in the understanding of Islam. He instituted and practiced the Five Pillars.

After Muhammad's passing, a group of visitors went to his widow, Aisha. They asked her, "What was the Prophet, God's Messenger, like?" "Have you read the Koran?" she replied. "He was the living Koran."

OTHER PROPHETS

Adam, the first human being, was the first prophet as well. God taught Adam all the Names, the essence of everything in creation: that is, God placed the seeds of all wisdom within humanity. We can find within ourselves all that we want and need.

Sufis consider Jesus to be one of the greatest prophets that God has sent and call him the Spirit of God. But God has blown Divine Spirit into the spirit of all human beings, beginning with Adam. We all contain God's Divine Spirit; however, that Spirit manifests fully only in the great prophets and Divine Messengers.

Sufis love and respect Moses as much as they do Jesus. Moses is known as the one who talks with God. According to an old Sufi story, one day some of the children of Israel went up to Moses and said, "You talk to God. Please tell him that we want to invite him to dinner." Moses became extremely angry. He said that God does not eat or come to dinner. But the next time Moses went up to Mt. Sinai, God said to him, "Why didn't you inform me of my dinner invitation from my servants?" Moses said, "But my Lord, You don't eat. You don't answer foolish invitations like this." God replied, "Keep what you know between you and Me. Tell them that I will come in answer to their invitation."

So Moses came down from Mt. Sinai and announced that God was coming to dinner after all. Of course, they all, including Moses, prepared an incredible feast. While they were busy cooking the finest dishes and preparing everything, an old man unexpectedly showed up. He was poor and hungry, and he asked for something to eat. The busy cooks said, "No, no, we are waiting for God. When God comes, we will all eat. Why don't you make yourself useful and help fetch water from the well?" They gave nothing to this poor man. Time passed, but God did not appear. Moses became terribly embarrassed and did not know what to tell everyone.

The next day Moses went up on Mt. Sinai and said, "God, what are you doing to me? I'm trying to convince everybody that you exist. You said you would come to our feast, and then you never showed up. Nobody is going to believe me anymore!" God replied, "But I did come. If you had fed my poor servant, you would have fed me."

God said, "I, who cannot be fit into all the universes, fit into the heart of my believing servant." When you serve one of God's servants, you serve God. Not only the prophets, but also the saints can be called God's servants. The general principle is that when you serve the created, you serve the Creator.

THE FOUR STAGES OF SUFISM

There are four stages of practice and understanding in Sufism— *shariah* (religious law), *tariqah* (the mystical path), *haqiqah* (Truth), and *marifah* (Gnosis). Each is built upon the stages that go before.

First is the *shariah,* which is the basic foundation for the next three stages. The *shariah* consists of teachings of Islam, basically the morality and ethics found in all religions. It provides guidance to us for living properly in this world. Trying to follow Sufism without following the *shariah* is like trying to build a house on a foundation of sand. Without an ordered life built on solid moral and ethical principles, mysticism cannot flourish. In Arabic, *shariah* means "road." It is a clear track, a well-traveled route that anyone can follow.

Second is the *tariqah,* which refers to the practice of Sufism. *Tariqah* literally means the path in the desert that the Bedouin would follow to travel from oasis to oasis. This path is not clearly marked like a highway; it is not even a visible road. To find your way in the trackless desert, you need to know the area intimately, or you need a guide who knows the destination and is familiar with the local landmarks. Just as the *shariah* refers to the external dimension of religion, the *tariqah* refers to the inner practices of Sufism. The guide you need in order to find your way is the sheikh, or Sufi teacher. The *shariah* makes the outer day-to-day life clean and attractive. The *tariqah* is designed to make the inner life clean and pure. Each of these supports the other.

Third is *haqiqah,* or Truth. *Haqiqah* refers to the inner meaning of the practices and guidance found in the *shariah* and *tariqah.* It is the direct experience of the mystical states of Sufism, direct experience of the presence of God within. Without this experience, seekers follow blindly, attempting to imitate those who know, those who have attained the station of *haqiqah.* The attainment of *haqiqah* confirms and solidifies the practice of the first two stages. Before *haqiqah* all practice is imitation. Without the deep inner understanding that comes from experience, one follows mechanically the teachings and practices of others.

Fourth is *marifah,* or Gnosis. Gnosis is superior wisdom or knowledge of spiritual truth. This is a deep level of inner knowing, beyond *haqiqah.* More than momentary spiritual experience, *marifah* refers to an ongoing state of attunement with God and with Truth. It is the knowledge of Reality, attained by a very few. This is the station of the Messengers, the prophets, and the great sages and saints.

The great Sufi sage Ibn 'Arabi explained these four levels as follows: At the level of the law *(shariah)* there is "yours and mine." That is, the law guarantees individual rights and ethical relations between people. At the level of the Sufi path *(tariqah),* "mine is yours and yours is mine." The dervishes are expected to treat one another as brothers and sisters—to open their homes, their hearts, and their purses to one another. At the level of Truth *(haqiqah),* there is "no mine and no yours." The advanced Sufis at this level realize that all things are from God, that they are really only caretakers and that they "possess" nothing. Those who realize Truth have gone beyond attachment to possessions and beyond attachment to externals in general, including fame and position. At the level of Gnosis *(marifah),* there is "no me and no you." At this final level, the individual has realized that all is God, that nothing and no one is separate from God.

What is lawful at one level may not be lawful at another level of understanding. For example, the outer practice of fasting is required by religious law, but according to the Sufi path, one of the essential reasons for fasting is to develop self-discipline and to control the insatiable ego. If a person is proud of fasting, the fast is still technically lawful, but in terms of the Sufi path, the fast is a failure.

Another example comes from the famous story of Mansur al-Hallaj, who was killed for publicly saying, *"Ana al Haqq,"* "I am Truth." One of the ninety-nine Attributes of God is Truth, and, according to the law, it is absolutely forbidden to call oneself God. The traditional punishment for this extreme heresy was death. However, from the point of view of Truth, the Divine is within each person; it dwells in one's heart of hearts. The innermost heart does have Divine qualities, and each person should be honored as a temple of God. As the Sufi saint Junaid replied when he was asked about Mansur, "What should he have said, 'I am Falsehood'?"

Opening the Heart

Love. For the great Sufi teacher and poet Rumi, love is the only force that can transcend the bounds of reason, the distinctions of knowledge, and the isolation of normal consciousness. The love he experienced was not only sensual pleasure; it might be more fully described as love for all things, for creation itself. Love is a continually expanding capacity that culminates in certainty, in the recognition that there is nothing in this world or in the next that is not both loved and loving.

> Thou didst contrive this "I" and "we" in order that
> Thou mightest play the game of worship with Thyself,
> That all "I's" and "thou's" should become one soul and
> at last should be submerged in the Beloved.
>
> *Rumi*

The perception of God as the Beloved, common to both Christian and Sufi writings, comes from direct experience. Sheikh Muzaffer, my own Sufi master, has written, "The essence of God is love and the Sufi path is a path of love. . . . Love is to see what is good and beautiful in everything. It is to learn from everything, to see the gifts of God and the generosity of God in everything. It is to be thankful for all God's bounties."

The Sufis report that by channeling their energy into loving God, they receive a response, that of being loved in return, just as in a personal relationship the act of loving brings forth or awakens love in another. In Sufism, it is said that if you take two steps toward God, God runs to you.

Love brings the lover to union with the beloved.

I've spent my life, my heart
And my eyes this way.
I used to think that love
And beloved are different.
I know now they are the same.
I was seeing two in one.

Rumi

At a certain point along the path of love, God reaches out and begins to assist us, drawing the seeker toward the divine presence. As this occurs, striving melts into surrender, through which one is helped to awaken, is taken in by God. Sheikh Muzaffer explains:

The eyes of the dervish who is a true lover see nought but God; his heart knows nought but Him. God is the eye by which he sees, the hand with which he holds, and the tongue with which he speaks. . . . Were he not in love, he would pass away. If his heart should be devoid of love for as much as a single moment, the dervish could not stay alive. Love is the dervish's life, his health, his comfort. Love ruins the dervish, makes him weep; union makes him flourish, brings him to life.

Remembrance. One of the basic Sufi practices to open the heart is remembrance. Abu-Hamid al-Ghazâli, in his book *Invocations and Supplications,* notes that remembrance has four basic meanings. First, it is an act of constantly striving to be mindful of God. In this sense, it is the opposite of heedlessness. Prayer is also remembrance. Prayer invites the Sufi into God's presence.

Second, remembrance is the repetition of a mystical formula or Divine Name, such as "There is no god but God," "Allah," "Life [*ya Hayy*]," or "Truth [*ya Haqq*]." This practice of invocation requires sincerity of intention, awareness, concentration, instruction, and authorization or initiation into the practice. This repetition is the remembrance of the tongue.

Third, remembrance means a temporary, inner state in which awareness of God overwhelms the person and he or she becomes truly divorced from all concerns for the world, at least for the moment. This is the remembrance of the heart.

Fourth, remembrance is a deep and stable inner station in which invocation and mindfulness have become constant. This is the remembrance of the soul.

The dervishes of most orders come together weekly to perform the ceremony of Remembrance of God. In the ceremony they invoke God by chanting and repeating God's Names. There are ninety-nine Names, or Divine Attributes, of God revealed in the Holy Koran. In addition to those mentioned above, they include Merciful, Eternal, Ever-living, Peace, Strength, Glory, and Power. Each order has been given, through dreams and visions, the right to use certain of these Names. As the dervishes call on God, they also begin to remember the Divine within themselves.

The Sufis attempt to practice unity of breath, sound, and movement in the Remembrance ceremony. Unity among the dervishes can bring them closer to God, Who *is* Unity. Ideally, the dervishes move as if there were only one dervish moving, chant as if one dervish were chanting, and breathe as if just one dervish were breathing.

During the ceremony, remembrance descends from the tongue to the heart and from the heart to the soul. In Arabic, the term for remembrance means both repetition and remembrance. The remembrance of the tongue is the beginning and is often just mechanical repetition. As the meaning and power of the words repeated begin to sink in, hearts become filled with joy, longing for

God, and other spiritual feelings. This state is the remembrance of the heart. Longing for God is also a sign of God's Presence within. Longing itself is a sign of God's Presence. This state is the remembrance of the soul.

The Prophet said,

God has made a polish for everything that tarnishes.
And the polish for the heart is remembrance.

The Sufis believe that before the material universe was created, we were all souls in the world of souls. God addressed the souls, "Am I not your Lord?" And they answered, "Yes, indeed!" The Sufis remember that state, in which they knew who they were, they knew God, and they were close to God.

LIVING IN THE WORLD

One basic Sufi principle is to live in the world and still pursue the highest mystical goals. To serve others is, in a real sense, to serve God, and this service is considered by many saints to be the highest form of worship. It is not enough simply to love or to know. We have to *act* on our love and our knowledge.

Love and Service. To be a dervish is to love and serve others. The dervishes seek to love one another, to speak kindly, to show gentleness to one another, and also to serve one another. That is actually the duty of the human being.

There are two conditions required of every dervish. One is to remember Who has created us, to praise God and be thankful to God. The other is to serve God's creation, starting with human beings first, but also animals and plants. God says in the Holy Koran that the best of human beings are the ones who are useful to others.

Worshiping God is the dervish's duty, and service is a form of worship. Service to creation brings the dervish close to God. Every dervish, just like other people, has worldly duties to perform. Dervishes have to take care of others and have to work. Dervishes work and serve others for God's sake, and then that work becomes worship. Generally, those who serve the most make the greatest progress on the Sufi path.

Through service as worship the individual comes closer to God. The highest state for any human being is to be found worthy of becoming God's servant and an instrument through which God serves creation. God has said, through Muhammad, "When I love a servant, I, the Lord, am his ear so that he hears by Me, I am his eye so that he sees by Me, and I am his tongue so that he speaks by Me, and I am his hand so that he takes by Me."

Service comes from love. Loving others inspires the Sufis to serve them well. God bequeathed these beautiful attributes of love and service to humankind, and nothing in the whole world is as sweet and uplifting as these wonderful qualities. By first striving to be God's servants, the Sufis then serve God's creation. Even giving water to plants is an example of this kind of service.

Some poor people once asked Hazreti 'Ali, the son-in-law of the Prophet, how they might help others. They had no money or food to spare. He told them to smile at others, to do their best to make other people feel cared for.

A group of Italians came to our Sufi center in Istanbul several years ago. A year later most of them returned. They were neither dervishes nor Muslims, but they said that the kindness and the smiling faces of everyone in the center brought them back. A kind, happy expression is a reflection of the contented heart of the dervish.

What is better, to love or to be loved? This is a question that is worthy of contemplation.

For the Sufi, the answer is to love. Because, if you love others, you will be loved by them in return. True lovers are always loved. The aim of the Sufi is to be accepted as a lover by the Beloved, that is, by God.

In a teaching by Attar, a Sufi saint meets a woman at the seashore and asks her, "What is the end of love?" She answers, "O simpleton, love has no end." He asks, "Why?" And she replies, "Because the Beloved has no end."

Gratitude. The best way to express gratitude to God is to worship God. God conceived this incredibly varied creation and chose to give people this human form. God might have chosen any form. Humankind cannot thank God enough for creating humanity in a human form, not even by worshiping God day and night.

When a group of guests thanked Sheikh Safer for his hospitality, he said,

> We must thank God. For if God had not wished it so, we would not have been here, you would not have been here, and we would not have met. It is God's generosity that we are here and that we are together. Obviously it has been in your destiny that you will share something to eat with us. This is the material side of things. The most basic aspect of this is that we have been able to share the same space. At the same time you have witnessed prayer and the ceremony of *dhikr*, the remembrance of God. So we have also shared in something spiritual.
>
> We also are thankful. When we begin our prayers, after we say, *"Allah hu ekber,"* "God is Greater," we say, *"Bismillah ir-rahmân ir-rahîm,"* "In the Name of God, the Merciful, the Compassionate." Then we say, *"Al hamdu 'lillah,"* "All praise is to God." That is how the prayer starts. That is how Sufis try to live.

TRANSFORMING THE SELF

The goal of all mysticism is to cleanse the heart, to educate, or transform, the self, and to find God. The lowest level of the self is dominated by pride, egotism, and totally self-centered greed and lust. This level is the part within each person that leads away from Truth. The highest level is the pure self, and at this level there is no duality, no separation from God.

The self is actually a living process rather than a static structure in the psyche. The self is not a thing. The Arabic term is related to words for "breath," "soul," "essence," "self," and "nature." It refers to a process that comes about from the interaction of body and soul.

When the soul becomes embodied, it forgets its original nature and becomes enmeshed in material creation. This creates the self.

The lowest level of the self, the ego or lower personality, is made up of impulses, or drives, to satisfy desires. These drives dominate reason or judgment and are defined as the forces in one's nature that must be brought under control. The self is a product of the self-centered consciousness—the ego, the "I." The self must be transformed—this is the ideal. The self is like a wild horse; it is powerful and virtually uncontrollable. As the self becomes trained, or transformed, it becomes capable of serving the individual. Sheikh Muzaffer has written,

> The self is not bad in itself. Never blame your self. Part of the work of Sufism is to change the state of your self. The lowest state is that of being completely dominated by your wants and desires. The next state is to struggle with yourself, to seek to act according to reason and higher ideals and to criticize yourself when you fail. A much higher state is to be satisfied with whatever God provides for you, whether it means comfort or discomfort, fulfillment of physical needs or not.

According to many Sufi teachers, there are seven levels of the self. They are seven levels of development, ranging from absolutely self-centered and egotistical to purely spiritual.

The Commanding Self. The first level has also been described as the domineering self or the self that incites to evil. The commanding self seeks to dominate and to control each individual. At this level there is unbridled selfishness and no sense of morality or compassion.

Descriptions of this level of self are similar to descriptions of the id in psychoanalytic theory; it is closely linked to lust and aggression. These have been called the swine and the dogs of the self—the sensual traits are like swine, the ferocious ones like fierce dogs or wolves. Wrath, greed, sensual appetites, passion, and envy are examples of traits at this level of the self. This is the realm of physical and egoistic desires.

At this level people are like addicts who are in denial. Their lives are dominated by uncontrollable addictions to negative traits and habits, yet they refuse to believe they have a problem. They have no hope of change at this level, because they do not acknowledge any need to change.

The Regretful Self. People who have not developed beyond the first level are unaware and unconscious. As the light of faith grows, insight dawns, perhaps for the first time. The negative effects of a habitually self-centered approach to the world become apparent to the regretful self.

At this level, wants and desires still dominate, but now the person repents from time to time and *tries* to follow higher impulses. As Sheikh Muzaffer points out,

> There is a battle between the self, the lower self, and the soul. This battle will continue through life. The question is, Who will educate whom? Who will become the master of whom? If the soul becomes the master, then you will be a believer, one who embraces Truth. If the lower self becomes master of the soul, you will be one who denies Truth.

At this second level, people do not yet have the ability to change their way of life in a significant way. However, as they see their faults more clearly, their regret and desire for change grow. At this level, people are like addicts who are beginning to realize the extent of their addiction and just beginning to understand the pain they have caused themselves and others. The addiction is still far too strong to change. That requires far stronger medicine.

The Inspired Self. At the next level, the seeker begins to take genuine pleasure in prayer, meditation, and other spiritual activities. Only now does the individual taste the joys of spiritual experience. Now the seeker is truly motivated by ideals such as compassion, service, and moral values. This is the beginning of the real practice of Sufism. Before this stage, the best anyone can accomplish is superficial outer understanding and mechanical outer worship.

Though one is not free of desires and ego, this new level of motivation and spiritual experience significantly reduces the power of these forces for the first time. What is essential here is to *live* in terms of higher values. Unless these new motivations become part of a way of life, they will wither and die away. Behaviors common to the inspired self include gentleness, compassion, creative acts, and moral action. Overall, a person who is at the stage of the inspired self seems to be emotionally mature, respectable, and respected.

The Contented Self. The seeker is now at peace. The struggles of the earlier stages are basically over. The old desires and attachments are no longer binding. The ego-self begins to let go, allowing the individual to come more closely in contact with the Divine.

This level of self predisposes one to be liberal, grateful, trusting, and adoring. If one accepts difficulties with the same overall sense of security with which one accepts benefits, it may be said that one has attained the level of the contented self. Developmentally, this level marks a period of transition. The self can now begin to "disintegrate" and let go of all previous concern with self-boundaries and then begin to "reintegrate" as an aspect of the universal self.

The Pleased Self. At this stage the individual is not only content with his or her lot, but pleased with even the difficulties and trials of life, realizing that these difficulties come from God. The state of the pleased self is very different from the way we usually experience the world, focused on seeking pleasure and avoiding pain. A Sufi story illustrates this:

Sultan Mahmud of Ghazna once shared a cucumber with Ayaz, his most loyal and beloved companion. Ayaz happily ate his half of the cucumber, but when the sultan bit into *his* half, it was so bitter he immediately spit it out.

"How could you manage to eat something so bitter?" the sultan exclaimed. "It tasted like chalk or like bitter poison!"

"My beloved sultan," answered Ayaz, "I have enjoyed so many favors and bounties from your hand that whatever you give me tastes sweet."

When a person's love and gratitude to God reach this level, he or she has reached the stage of the pleased self.

The Self Pleasing to God. Those who reach the next stage realize that all power to act comes from God, that they can do nothing by themselves. They no longer fear anything or ask for anything.

The Sufi sage Ibn 'Arabi describes this level as the inner marriage of self and soul. The self pleasing to God has achieved genuine inner unity and wholeness. At earlier stages, people struggle with the world because they experience multiplicity. A broken mirror creates a thousand different reflections of a single image. If the mirror could be made whole again, it would then reflect the single, unified image. By healing the multiplicity within, the Sufi experiences the world as whole and unified.

The Pure Self. Those few who attain the final level have transcended the self entirely. There is no ego or separate self left, only union with God. At this stage, the individual has truly realized the truth, "There is no god but God." The Sufi now knows that there is nothing but God, that only the Divine exists, and that any sense of individuality or separateness is an illusion.

Rumi illuminates this state for us:

> If you could get rid
> Of yourself just once,
> The secret of secrets
> Would open to you.
> The face of the unknown,
> Hidden beyond the universe
> Would appear on the
> Mirror of your perception.

THE ROLE OF THE TEACHER

A teacher is like a physician of the soul. Seekers need teachers because few have the knowledge of spiritual medicine they need to cure themselves and fewer still have the self-knowledge to diagnose themselves correctly. As one modern sheikh has put it, the transformation sought in Sufism requires the equivalent of a major operation. It might be possible to diagnose oneself and even treat simple problems, but one cannot operate on oneself. In another common metaphor, a teacher is a spiritual alchemist who can transform the dervish's soul into pure gold.

In the West, seekers are often attracted to those who write or speak beautifully about great truths. To discuss the truth and not live it is hypocrisy. Insincere teaching can weaken or even destroy a student's faith. A real Sufi teacher practices what he or she preaches. Empty words have no weight.

One day, a teacher was asked about patience. He spoke beautifully about patience with words full of wisdom. Just then, a scorpion stung his foot, not just once but repeatedly. However, he did not interrupt his talk, despite the pain.

When his listeners became aware of what had happened, they wondered why the teacher had not moved his foot away from the scorpion.

"I was discussing patience," he explained. "I could hardly give you any advice on that subject without setting an example of patience myself. I would have felt ashamed before God."

Although the sheikh is often referred to as the sun and the dervishes as planets, the sheikh is also like a mirror or a transmitter. That is, the light and blessings that flow from a sheikh are not his or her own. They come from God.

Sufi Orders. Every Sufi teacher has been authorized by his or her own teacher. This is why a Sufi order is referred to as a *silsila,* a chain. Each order contains an unbroken chain of sheikhs, each trained, initiated, and confirmed as a teacher by his or her own sheikh. This chain reaches all the way back to the prophet Muhammad, and through him to God. There are no self-appointed "masters" in Sufism.

The chain is also like a pipeline, in which each sheikh is a section of pipe. The blessings that come to each dervish flow through the pipeline. They flow *through* the sheikh, but they are not from the sheikh. A sheikh need not be perfect or all-knowing. What is important is that the section of pipe for which he or she is responsible is without holes and is tightly connected to the pipeline so that blessings can flow freely without leaking away.

The term for blessing, *baraka,* might also be translated as spiritual energy. Some sheikhs are said to have more than others. Visitors will often come to a teacher seeking blessings for their worldly affairs, and many people will go to pray at a saint's tomb, hoping that the *baraka,* or spiritual power, of the saint will help them.

A Sufi guide teaches students to move closer to realizing their inner nature. The guide teaches out of his or her own personal understanding and fullness of being. Teaching is in itself an expression of the Divine will.

Students often underwent a long period of testing and discipline before becoming accepted as a dervish. For example, in the Mevlevi Order, which was founded by Rumi, the novice served in the kitchen, studied Rumi's writings, and practiced the technique of turning (popularly known as whirling). This training traditionally continued for 1,001 days.

Four major attributes of a sheikh are maturity, patience, awareness of the student, and being in the world while free of the world.

Maturity. A Persian phrase beautifully illustrates this aspect of a teacher. "The sheikh is a mature ['cooked'] person who knows the world." That is, a teacher is an experienced and mature human being, who appreciates the pitfalls and temptations of the world, who understands others, and who also knows the spiritual path. Because the teacher knows the world, he or she can understand all aspects of the dervish's life.

Patience. The great Sufi saint and philosopher Ibn 'Arabi was asked by his teacher to explain the meaning of this verse from the

Koran: "I require no provision from them, nor do I need them to feed Me." Ibn 'Arabi thought for a while and then left without a word.

At that time, Ibn 'Arabi was already a famous scholar with a reputation for his own understanding and interpretations of the verses of the Koran. He realized that his sheikh was asking for a deeper level of interpretation than he was capable of at that time, so he left and meditated on the verse for four years. Four years later, when he returned to his sheikh, the first thing his teacher said was, "Give me your answer. After four years, the time is ripe for it."

Patience is essential for both teacher and student. It is one of the Divine Names, or Attributes, and it is mentioned more often in the Koran than any other. A common Sufi metaphor for patience is that of ripened fruit. Unripe fruit tastes bitter and may cause indigestion. When the fruit ripens, it will become sweet and nourishing, and its ripened seeds will have the potential for rebirth.

The saint Shibli once tested the sincerity and patience of his students. When Shibli entered a profound mystical state, he was locked up as a madman. Many of his students went to visit him, and when they arrived, Shibli asked, "Who are you?"

"We are some of those who love and follow you."

Shibli began throwing stones at his visitors. Stung by the stones, they began to run away, crying, "It is true—Shibli really has gone crazy!"

Then Shibli called out to them, "Didn't I hear you say that you loved me? You could not even bear a stone or two before running away. What became of that sincere love you claimed you had for me? Did your love fly away with a couple of stones? If you really loved me, you would have patiently endured the little bit of discomfort I caused you."

Awareness of the Student. Real teachers are intuitively aware of the inner state and inner thoughts of their students. The teacher serves as a mirror in which the students can see themselves. In many ways the relationship between sheikh and dervish is similar to the relationship between psychotherapist and client. There is often an intense emotional connection, as well as deep inner insight. Most psychotherapy is based on the assumption that the client or patient needs help, and the goal is to strengthen the ego so that the patient can function more effectively in society. The goal of the relationship with the sheikh is to strengthen the dervish's connection with the soul and deepen the dervish's remembrance of God.

Being in the World but Not of It. In many orders, the sheikhs are expected to have jobs, marry, raise children, and serve their communities. Work, marriage, and raising a family can be essential elements in the development of maturity.

A man once questioned Sigmund Freud about healthy, normal people. He complained that almost all Freud wrote about was neurosis and mental illness, and he asked Freud to describe the characteristics of a mature and healthy human being. Freud answered simply and elegantly, "Love and work." To describe a sheikh, we might add, "Love, work, service, and remembrance of God."

The teacher knows how to deal effectively with daily reality and yet not lose sight of the Divine. Sufi teachers have been artisans, merchants, fishermen, and shopkeepers. Many of the greatest teachers have had lowly jobs, such as porters, water carriers, and janitors.

Many great sheikhs have been advisers to rulers and to the wealthy and powerful yet were never influenced by wealth, power, or glory. There is an old Sufi saying that even if a sheikh visits a sultan, the sultan is the sheikh's guest, the sheikh is never the sultan's guest. That is, the sheikh visits in order to serve and to benefit the sultan, just as a good host serves a guest. The sheikh does not seek any gain or benefit from the sultan.

Many years ago the sultan of the Ottoman Empire visited one of the great sheikhs of Istanbul. He was deeply impressed with the wisdom and sincerity of the sheikh and began coming regularly to the sheikh's gatherings. After some time the sultan said, "I have come to love you and your teachings. If there is anything you want or need, please ask me and I will provide it for you if it is in my power." This was, in effect, a blank check from one of the wealthiest and most powerful men on earth.

The sheikh replied, "Yes, there is one thing you can do for me. Please do not come back." The astonished sultan asked, "Have I done anything to offend you? If so, please accept my apologies." The sheikh replied, "No, the problem is not you; it is my dervishes. Before you began visiting us, they would pray and chant to God, seeking only God's blessings. Now, their minds are occupied with thoughts of pleasing you and receiving a reward from you. I have to ask you not to come back, because we are not spiritually mature enough to handle your presence here."

The Recollection of Death

Contemplating death can be a powerful tool for releasing an individual from undesirable habits and attitudes. Thinking about one's own death is an exercise in becoming more aware of one's present experiences. Confronting mortality is one way of beginning the process of personal growth. Until recently Western society has avoided awareness of death. The West has developed a death-fearing culture.

The following exercise from al-Ghazzali will engrave the awareness of death into your consciousness:

Remember your contemporaries who have passed away, and were of your age.

Remember the honors and fame they earned, the high posts they held and the beautiful bodies they possessed, and today all of them are turned to dust.

How they have left orphans and widows behind them.

No sign of them is left today, and they lie in the dark holes underneath the earth.

Picture their faces before your mind's eye and ponder.

Do not fix hopes on your wealth and do not laugh away life. Remember how they walked and now all their joints lie separated and the tongue with which they talked lightly is eaten away by the worms and their teeth are corroded. They were foolishly providing for twenty years when even a day of their lives was not left. They never expected that death shall come to them thus at an unexpected hour.

Some years ago, two patients were scheduled for operations in a major hospital in Istanbul. One was a young man with a minor case of appendicitis, and the other was an old man with cancer. The same surgeon operated on both. The appendix operation was extremely simple and was over quickly. When the doctor opened up the man with cancer, he saw that the cancer had spread so much it was inoperable, and so he simply closed up the incision.

The doctor commented that the young man probably had many more years to live but that the old man would not last very long at all. That night, the young man died, and a few days later the old man left the hospital. Months later, the old man returned to the hospital bringing fresh fruits and vegetables from his garden as a present for the doctor. At first the doctor didn't recognize him, then the old man reminded him that he was the cancer patient on whom the doctor had operated the same day that a young man had died.

None of us knows how much time we have. The strong and healthy among us may think they have many years left, but death can come at any time. And even with a serious illness, like cancer, it should be remembered that, if God wills, we may still have many years to live.

Developing two important attitudes helps prepare one for death. One is that death is inevitable. Everyone dies. This life has only so many more minutes, days, months, or years. Remembering that, one will live more consciously and responsibly than thinking that there is infinite time to put things in order.

The second attitude is to remember that no one knows *when* the time will come. It might come in the next moment, or it may come many years from now, but no one knows, and there are no guarantees. Somehow people seem to think that death will pass them by until they are ready for it, until things are "in order." But that is not the way life works. Most people die in the middle of their busy lives, with all their plans and activities unfinished.

Before he passed on, the Prophet told his Companions, "I will leave you with two teachers after I am gone—a speaking teacher and a silent teacher. The speaking teacher is the Koran. The silent teacher is death."

How to Use This Book

This book contains a wealth of stories, anecdotes, and poetry. If you try to absorb it all at once, you are likely to develop intellectual indigestion. Instead, read a little at a time, or skim, letting your eyes run over several pages until you come to a passage or a poem that strikes you. You might make a check mark or write a short note in the margin beside those pieces that touch you.

I have found that many of the stories and prose passages in this book have dropped quietly into my memory to resurface when needed. Years ago, I went on *hajj* (pilgrimage), visiting Mecca and Medina with two and a half million other pilgrims. In Medina, we would get up before dawn and go to the main mosque. The mosque was much smaller then than it is now, and most pilgrims prayed in an annex next to the mosque. What seemed like acres of land were covered to protect us from the sun.

Each morning, while it was still dark, I would find a place in the annex. The covering was rippled sheet metal that would come to a peak at one cross beam and then down to a "V" at the next. The roof itself seemed to ripple. At each "V" there was a neon strip and a large ceiling fan moving slowly. These individual elements might seem pedestrian or even ugly, but somehow each morning, before dawn, there was a subtle, unearthly beauty in the row after row of lights and fans.

Over one million people came to pray in this annex every morning. Once prayers were over, there was an incredible rush to get out. Everyone wanted to get back to their rooms or to a food stand for a bite to eat. There was a tremendous amount of pushing and shoving as people from cultures that don't respect orderly lines kept forcing themselves forward.

For the first few days I got caught up in pushing and shoving myself. I was bigger than most other pilgrims and had practiced martial arts for more than twenty years. I pushed and shoved with the best of them. The third day it dawned on me: here I was on pilgrimage, acting like a bully. Suddenly lines that I'd read in a Sufi collection entitled *Intimate Conversations* came back to me. They'd had little impact when I'd first read them, but now they struck me with tremendous force:

> To be a dervish means to be a lump of sifted earth
> with a little water sprinkled on top.
> It means to be something that
> neither harms the soles of the feet
> nor leaves a trail of dust behind.

The rest of my pilgrimage was transformed. I let myself flow with the crowds, and wherever I could, I yielded instead of pushing. I actively sought to do no harm to anyone or anything, in spite of the stress of milling crowds, incredible heat, and an exhausting schedule. These few lines made a huge difference.

I know that many of the other passages in this book have the same potential to awaken and to change us. I hope they will touch you as they have touched me.

PART 1

The Many Faces of Sufism

CHAPTER 1

The Sufi Way

The Sufi way is not a path of retreat from the world but a way of seeking the Divine while still actively engaged in the world. Engagement in the world provides opportunities for spiritual growth, opportunities to practice love, awareness, generosity, and nonattachment. The Sufi approach is summarized by Sheikh Muzaffer, a modern Sufi teacher: "Keep your hands busy with your duties in this world, and your heart busy with God."

Our hearts have become frozen, armored against the pain and suffering we have all experienced in this world. With the help of a devoted teacher and sincere brothers and sisters along the path, we can defrost them.

Love, service, and compassion help us reopen our hearts and come closer to God. One of the greatest services we can perform is to help heal the injured hearts of others. Our hands are made to lift up those who have fallen, to wipe the tears of those who are suffering from the trials of this world. Sheikh Muzaffer also said, "A kind word or glance softens your heart, and every hurtful word or act closes or hardens your heart."

There is a wisdom of the heart far different from the wisdom of the head. The head can be misled by appearances; the wise heart sees beyond outer forms to inner reality. As one Sufi master explained Sufism, "Anyone can learn the outer forms of prayer and worship. Sufism seeks to develop a heart that can pray." The stories, poetry, and prose that follow are from those who developed heart's wisdom. May their words touch our hearts as well.

⌒

The Sufi is absent from himself and present with God.

Hujwiri

The Sufis are those who have preferred God to everything, so that God has preferred them to everything.

Dhu-l-Nun

We Sufis are lovers of beauty. Because we have renounced the world, it does not mean that we should look miserable. But neither do we want to stand out and attract undue attention. . . . We behave like others, we dress like others. We are ordinary people, living ordinary lives. We will always obey the law of the land in which we live; but in reality we are beyond the laws of men, for we obey only the law of God. We surrendered somewhere: we are completely free!

Irina Tweedie

If you are possessed of discernment joined with knowledge,
seek the company of the dervishes and become one with
      them.
Associate with none but them.
Love of the dervishes is the key that opens the door of
      Paradise.

Those who walk on the Path have no longing after fine
        palaces and fair gardens.
In their hearts is nothing but the pain of yearning love
        for God.

Junaid

The Sufis do not abandon this world, nor do they hold that
human appetites must be done away with. They only discipline
those desires that are in discordance with the religious life and
the dictates of sound reason.

They don't throw away all things of this world, nor do they
go after them with a vengeance. Rather, they know the true
value and function of everything upon the earth. They save as
much as is necessary. They eat as much as they need to stay
healthy.

They nourish their bodies and simultaneously set their
hearts free. God becomes the focal point toward which their
whole being leans. God becomes the object of their continual
adoration and contemplation.

al-Ghazzali

The thing we tell of can never be found by seeking, yet only
seekers find it.

Bayazid Bistami

Whatever you have in your mind—forget it; whatever you have
in your hand—give it; whatever is to be your fate—face it!

Abu Sa'id

The Sufi acts according to whatever is most fitting to the
moment.

Amr ibn Uthman al-Makki

The Sufi is he whose thought keeps pace with his foot.

He is entirely present; his soul is where his body is, and his body where his soul is, and his soul where his foot is, and his foot where his soul is.

Hujwiri

Today I am in such a shape
That I can't differentiate
The load from the donkey.
I am in such shape today,
That I don't know which is the thorn
And which is the rose.

My Love put me in this shape today.
I don't know who is the Lover
Or who is the Beloved.

Yesterday, drunkenness led me
To the door of the Love.
But today I can't find
The door or the house.

Last year I had two wings.
Fear and hope.
Today, I don't know of wings,
Don't know how to fly,
Don't know of my lost fears.

Rumi

The journey from this world to the next (to give up worldly things for spiritual things) is easy for the believer. The journey from the creatures to the Creator is hard. The journey from the self to God is very hard. And to be able to abide in God is harder still.

Junaid

Although there are some differences in the way things are done
in the lodges of other Sufi orders, in essence they are not very
different. *There is no lack of love or respect between these various
orders.* They do not reject each other, or criticize each other. Nor
do they claim to be closer to the Truth. Sometimes it is said,
"The fountain from which I drank was here, and there are many
other fountains if you are thirsty."

Murat Yagan

A seeker went to ask a sage for guidance on the Sufi way. The
sage counseled, "If you have never trodden the path of love, go
away and fall in love; then come back and see us."

Jami

"I" and "you" are but the lattices,
In the niches of a lamp
Through which the One Light shines.
"I" and "you" are the veil
Between heaven and earth;
Lift this veil and you will see
No longer the bonds of sects and creeds.

Shabistari

If words come out of the heart, they will enter the heart, but if
they come from the tongue, they will not pass beyond the ears.

al-Suhrawardi

Whoever hears something of the Sufi doctrine *and practices it,* it
becomes wisdom in their hearts, and people who listen to them
will derive benefit from it. Whoever hears and does not practice,
Sufism is mere talk which they will forget after a few days.

al-Suhrawardi

You will not be a mystic until you are like the earth—both the righteous and the sinner tread upon it—and until you are like the clouds—they shade all things—and until you are like the rain—it waters all things, whether it loves them or not.

Bayazid Bistami

God's favor comes unexpectedly,
but only to an alert heart.
Put not your hope in people,
for you will be wounded.

Put your hope in God
that you may be delivered.

Ansari

The perfect mystic is neither an ecstatic devotee lost in contemplation of Oneness nor a saintly recluse shunning all commerce with mankind. The true saint goes in and out among the people, eats and sleeps with them, buys and sells in the market, marries and takes part in social intercourse, and never forgets God for a single moment.

Abu Sa'id

A man once insulted the sage Jafar al-Sadiq. Sometime later Jafar went to the man's house and addressed him:

"When you said certain things to me, I made no reply. If the qualities you attribute to me are really in me, I give you my word that I shall repent of them and not let myself be guilty of them again, but if the qualities you ascribed to me are not really in me, I shall pray to God and beseech Him to pardon you. I forgive you what you said to me and do not hold it against you."

This kindness made such an impression on the man that he fell at the feet of the sage and repented.

Sheikh Muzaffer

It is necessary to have a guide for the spiritual journey. Choose a master, for without one this journey is full of trials, fears, and dangers. With no escort, you would be lost on a road you have already taken. Do not travel alone on the Path.

Rumi

PART 2

Living in the World

CHAPTER 2

Daily Life

A scrim is a piece of stage scenery on which the background of a set is painted. When lit from the front, it is opaque and creates the illusion of being whatever the play demands: a wall, a street, a mountain range, a view of paradise. But when lit from behind, it becomes transparent, almost invisible, and the actual stage behind it can be seen.

This world is like a scrim, a temporary creation, beyond which can be seen the stage on which (at another time) other plays will be mounted and other actors will perform their parts. We tend to see the world as if it were solid, permanent, and substantial. Seen through the eyes of Truth, however, it becomes transparent. When our vision pierces the scrim, we begin to see life as it is, through the eyes of the Creator. Only then can we view the real universe.

There are, it is said, seventy thousand veils between ourselves and God. These are habits and ideas that prevent us from remembering and being aware of our direct connection with the Divine. Each time we pierce a veil, we come a little closer to our own spiritual center. Each time a painted image deludes us, we drift farther away from ourselves.

The task before the Sufi is twofold: first, to develop the ability to recognize and remember the Truth; second, to help others to do the same. As one evolves, the two tasks merge and become, ultimately, the same.

Look to what you do,
for that is what you are worth.
True labor means neither fasting nor prayer.

Ansari

A man was passing a mental hospital. He called out to one of the patients peering through the windows, "How many madmen are there in the hospital?" Looking the questioner up and down, the inmate replied, "Why don't you leave us alone? But tell me, how many sane people are there out there?" The precondition is to know yourself. He who does not know cannot find, and he who does not find cannot be.

Sheikh Muzaffer

The Sultan Mustafa III asked a saint, "What are the pleasures of this world?" The saint replied, "To eat, drink, and break wind." This answer annoyed the sultan, who dismissed the saint from his presence. The saint cursed him, saying, "My Emperor, may you eat and drink but nothing more." And so it happened. The sultan ate and drank but was unable to excrete. Naturally his discomfort got worse by the day. Despite the attentions of all the doctors, nothing relieved his condition. Finally, he sent for the holy man and begged him for relief. The saint said, "If you will give me your empire, I will let you break wind once." What could the wretched sultan do but agree? His life was ebbing away. The saint put his hands on the sultan's stomach and stroked it once. The monarch broke wind and heaved a sigh of relief. "You see, my Emperor," said the saint, "I have bought your empire for the price of a single fart."

Sheikh Muzaffer

The soul should take care of the body, just as the pilgrim on his way to Mecca takes care of his camel; but if the pilgrim spends his whole time in feeding and adorning his camel, the caravan will leave him behind, and he will perish in the desert.

al-Ghazzali

Man may be asleep, but he must awake in the right way. One necessity is that when he is awake, he will also have the means to profit by his wakefulness.

Idries Shah

It is reported that 'Ali Sahl once wrote a letter to Junaid in which he declared that sleep is a form of negligence. The letter went on to declare that if a lover sleeps he is hindered in his goal and will become negligent about himself. In reply, Junaid wrote, "Our conscious effort to stay awake is a business transaction on the way to God, whereas our sleep is the active volition of God upon us. Therefore, it can be said that whatever happens from God in the absence of our conscious choice is better than what we ourselves choose in order to reach Him."

Junaid

Sufis are absorbed somewhere all the time; they don't notice good or bad. We should be able to sleep in the street when there is no other possibility. Why not? The street is also a part of Him, made by Him. Sufis don't say, "I do this or that." THEY DO IT.

Irina Tweedie

Once there was a King, who was interested in music and dancing and drama and higher education. He told his minister, "I want to hear good music and see dancing and dramatic performances. How can we arrange this?"

"May it please your Majesty, all the people in this country are accomplished musicians and actors and dancers, so that if we invite one group, we will offend another group. We must let it be known that there will be a competition six months from now and that the winners will get a prize from the King."

So a great stage was built in an open area of a thousand acres. The contest was announced, and everyone, down to the age of six months, started training themselves in music and acting.

On the appointed day, the huge space was filled with artists. There was a pavilion for the King and below it a small stage which would hold about twenty-five people, and all around that was the entire population of the country. The King asked the minister to blow the conch shell and tell the audience to stand to one side and the competitors on the other. It was done, and there was no audience. Everyone was a competitor! The King turned to the teacher seated beside him, "What shall I do?"

"Let them all dance and sing and act at once, and then decide who's the best." So they did, and the noise was horrendous. You couldn't distinguish one voice from another. It was like thousands of donkeys braying and foxes howling. . . .

In that same way God made the world, and everyone came with a billion different costumes and hypnotic illusion-projections, and the event got so chaotic and degraded and violent with all the competing religions and the complicated philosophical systems and the art-status titles, and with everyone aggressively pushing to be impressive, and with no one there like the King. The Kingdom of God is what there is to win, and that's within. It's very rare that someone comes and just watches with the King and so receives the prize within the King.

Bawa Muhaiyaddeen

Pray for what you want, but work for the things you need.

Modern traditional

A rider discovered a snake caught in the midst of a forest fire. When the snake saw him, it appealed for help, and because the rider was a God-fearing man, he overcame his fears and, holding out his saddlebag on the end of a spear, lifted the snake out of the fire. "Now go where you will," he said, "and in gratitude for your release, trouble mankind no more." But the snake turned on him, saying, "I shall not leave till I have killed you and your camel. You knew that I was a symbol of evil to men, and yet you ignored the proverb, 'Kindness to evil men is like injury to good men,' so you just take the consequences. Moreover, I am only copying the practice of men themselves." The rider protested and said, "If you can prove to me that this is the practice of men, I will accept my fate." Just then a buffalo appeared, and the snake asked him, "What is the reward of good?" "For years I raised calves for my master and gave him milk and butter, but now that I am old he plans to sell me to the butcher." The snake turned triumphantly to the rider, but the latter said, "According to law one witness is not enough." So the snake turned to a tree and asked, "What is the reward of good?" The tree replied, "According to the practice of men, it is evil. I give shade and rest to weary travelers, and then they tear off my branches to make shafts for axes and spades." The snake turned once more in triumph to the rider, but the latter said, "Life is dear to me. I beg you, find yet one more witness to support you, and then I will submit without question to my fate." The snake then noticed a fox who had been listening to the conversation, but before the question could be put to him, the fox cried out, "Of course the reward of good is evil. Now tell me, what good has the man done to the snake that he should be rewarded with evil?" The man told his story, and the fox asked the snake if he agreed. "Yes," was the reply, "and here is the bag in which he lifted me." "How ridiculous," said the fox, "you could not possibly fit into such a tiny bag." "I'll show you," replied the snake, and slid back into the bag. The fox cried out, "When you find your enemy in bonds, don't release him," and the rider, hastily closing the opening, beat the bag on the ground until the snake was dead.

Elwell Sutton

"Does money upset the hearts of learned men?" He answered, "Men whose hearts are changed by money are not learned."

al-Ghazzali

A merchant of Nishapur had lent some money to somebody living far away from his city. He wanted to go to that place to recover it. He had a beautiful girl in his service and could think of no one trustworthy enough to leave her with. Ultimately he decided to ask the pious saint Hadrat 'Uthman Hariri. It was only with much difficulty that he prevailed upon him to keep the girl with him during his absence.

One day Hariri's eyes accidentally fell on the girl, and he was infatuated with her. But he controlled himself. He went to his spiritual director Hadrat Abu Hafs Hadad and asked him to admonish his rebellious heart. The teacher advised him to go to Hadrat Yusef bin Hussain and follow his advice. When Hariri reached Yusef's town, the people warned him not to visit Yusef as he was turned into a heretic. Hariri returned home. When his teacher learned of this, he again asked Hariri to visit Yusef. This time he went to his house and was surprised to find him seated by a young beautiful boy with a jug of wine and a tumbler lying in front of them, yet Yusef's face shone bright like that of a saint. Hariri could not understand his unscriptural behavior, but he sat down in front of him.

When Yusef started the spiritual talk, his words were so effective that Hariri passed into ecstasy. When he recovered, he asked Yusef the reasons for his unorthodox behavior. Hussain said, "This boy is my son and is studying the Koran with me, and this flagon contains cold water. And as to your questions why I adopt such a queer behavior, this is to avoid any merchant entrusting me with his beautiful slave girl to be kept in my custody until his return."

Attar

A man once made this bequest to his son: "Take these hundred gold pieces, my son. You are to give them to the biggest fool you meet." The man died, and the son set out to discharge his father's bequest. Whenever he saw somebody acting stupidly, he would approach him to check whether he had found a fool.

In the course of his search, he came one day to a palace, in front of which a crowd had gathered. A bystander explained to him, "The Grand Vizier has displeased the Emperor. The executioner is going to behead him now, then the new Grand Vizier will be made to step over the dead body of his predecessor before being installed in his office." When asked the reason for this, he was told, "As an admonition to the incoming minister."

A moment later, they brought out a man in handcuffs. Ignoring his moans and groans, they forced him to his knees and cut off his head. The new minister witnessed this scene, then trod on the corpse of his executed predecessor to mount the Grand Vizier's throne of office. Everyone started congratulating the new minister. The young man mingled with the well-wishers. When he came in front of the Grand Vizier, he handed him the purse containing the gold pieces. "What is your motive in giving me this money?" "Please take it," said the youth. "It is a bequest of my late father's. Allow me to discharge my duty." The minister then asked, "Do you mean to tell me that your father's bequest was to give a hundred gold pieces to the Grand Vizier?" "No," replied the young man, "not to the Grand Vizier or minister. My father's bequest was to give money to a great fool. I have searched high and low, but—forgive me saying so—I have not come across a greater fool than you."

"How do you know I am a fool?" the minister asked, angrily. The young man explained: "I witnessed this ceremony with my own eyes. Your predecessor was beheaded just a short time ago, and you stepped over his body to mount this throne of office. The very same calamity could befall you tomorrow. One who saw this, yet took no warning from it, is not just any old fool; he is The Fool himself. Praise be to Allah, the bequest is fulfilled."

Sheikh Muzaffer

A man once came to the blessed Messenger, complaining that his father had spent all his money without asking his permission. Our Master called the man's father into his presence. When this very aged person arrived, leaning on his staff, he asked him, "Do you take your son's money without his permission?" "O Prophet of Allah," he cried, "once I was strong, while my son was weak; I was rich, while he was poor; and I didn't hoard my money but fed him, even when I did not eat. Now I have grown old and weak, while my son has grown strong. I have become poor, while he has become rich. He began to hide his money from me. I used to set his food in front of him, but he keeps his food to himself. I never have treated him as he treats me. If I were as strong as I used to be, I would not grudge him my money." At this, the blessed eyes of the Messenger brimmed with tears that fell like pearls upon his beard. "All right, father," he said, "Go and spend as much of your son's money as you wish; that money is yours."

Sheikh Muzaffer

If men had been forbidden to make porridge of camel's dung, they would have done it, saying that they would not have been forbidden to do it unless there had been some good in it.

Muhammad

No one who possesses snow would find any hardship in exchanging it for jewels and pearls. This world is like snow exposed to sun, which continues to melt until it disappears altogether, while the next life is like a precious stone that never passes away.

al-Ghazzali

An unjust king asked a devotee what kind of worship is best. He replied, "For thee the best is to sleep one half of the day so as not to injure the people for a while."

Sa'di

Everything in the world of existence has an end and a goal. The end is maturity, and the goal is freedom. For example, the fruit grows on the tree until it is ripe and then falls. A farmer sows grain in the ground and tends it. It begins to grow, eventually seeds, and again becomes grain. It has returned to its original form. The circle is complete. Completing the circle of existence is freedom.

Nasafi

A very close friend of Hamdun was on his deathbed. The sheikh was with him until his last breath. As the man died, Hamdun blew out the candle. The other people present exclaimed, "At a time like this, more light is called for!" He replied, "Before, the candle was his. Now it belongs to his heirs!"

Sheikh Hamdun

A man once went to the public steam bath, where he stretched out on a slab and fell asleep. In his sleep he dreamed. A person exactly resembling himself entered the bath, taking the cubicle opposite. This man was being treated like someone rich and important. The dreamer went up to the cubicle door to get a closer look. He saw that the individual had died in there. The thought occurred to him, "Suppose I change places with this fellow. If I swapped bath towels, I could pass for him." He put this thought into action. When masseurs came in and saw the dead body lying on the slab, they cried, "Help! This man has gone and died here." Then they carried him out.

Turning to the dreamer, they asked if he had sweated enough. He said that he had, so they washed him down and made him nice and clean. After leaving the bath, he went through the pockets of the dead man's clothes, which he was now wearing. They contained thousands of dollars. He got into the car that came to take the other man home and went to his apartment. There several gorgeous ladies came up to him, saying, "You must be tired after your bath, but please take these bank drafts. It seems you have made a big profit from your estate in such and such a place. They have sent the key to the villa you recently had built. And Madame would like to see you . . . "

At that moment, his face stinging from a hard slap, he found himself looking up at the scowling faces of the masseurs. "Get up, you loafer," they snarled. "You've been lying here since morning. The bath is closing." Then they threw him out into the street.

This man's state is similar to the condition of people who live in this world without faith. What they see is nothing but a dream. When the angels of death come for these people's souls, then they will realize they have nothing real!

Sheikh Muzaffer

I noticed an Arab of the desert sitting in a company of jewelers. He said: "I had once lost my road in the desert and consumed all my food. I considered that I must perish when I suddenly caught sight of a bulging canvas bag. I shall never forget the joy and ecstasy I felt on thinking it might be parched grain nor the bitterness and despair when I discovered it to be full of pearls."

Sa'di

Jesus (upon whom be peace!) saw the world revealed in the form of an ugly old hag. He asked her how many husbands she had possessed; she replied that they were countless. He asked whether they had died or been divorced; she said that she had slain them all. "I marvel," he said, "at the fools who see what you have done to others, and still desire you."

al-Ghazzali

The people of Reality say, "A sin committed with love is more meritorious than a loveless act of worship." For loveless worship is no more rewarded than a vain exertion. A sin committed with love will result in punishment, of course, but at least it is enjoyable. So whatever you do, do it with love!

Sheikh Muzaffer

Do not buy the enmity of one man for the love of a thousand men.

al-Ghazzali

It is related that Habib possessed a maidservant for thirty years. One day he said to the maid, "Hey veiled woman, go and call my maid." She replied, "But, sir, I am your maid. Don't you recognize me?" Habib answered, "During this time, I never dared to look at anything but Him, how then should I have recognized you?"

al-'Ajami

A man said to the Emissary of God (may God bless him and grant him peace), "Give me some advice." "Fear God," he replied, "wherever you may be." "Give me more," he said. "Follow a sin with a good deed," he replied.

Muhammad

This world is a place of preparation where one is given many lessons and passes many tests. Choose less over more in it. Be satisfied with what you have, even if it is less than what others have. In fact, prefer to have less.

This world is not bad—on the contrary, it is the field of the hereafter. What you plant here, you will reap there. This world is the way to eternal bliss and so is good—worthy to be cherished and to be praised.

What is bad is what you do with the world when you become blind to truth and totally consumed by your desires, lust, and ambition for it. Our master the Prophet (peace and blessings be upon him), in whom wisdom was as clear as crystal, was asked, "What is worldliness?" He answered, "Everything that makes you heedless and causes you to forget your Lord." Therefore the goods of this world are not harmful in themselves, but only when you let them render you forgetful, disobedient, and unaware of the Lord.

Ibn 'Arabi

CHAPTER 3

Self-Deception and Self-Knowledge

You cannot see the back of your own head, no matter how intently you stare into a mirror or how quickly you turn around. Even the most clear-sighted have blind spots. These places to which we ourselves are blind are often astonishingly visible to others.

The sword of self-knowledge, the ability to see oneself clearly, spans the abyss of ignorance. Below its stretched length blaze the swirling fires of ego while fogs of delusion and self-deception flow in from every side. In spite of the dangers, there is guidance to help us traverse that blade's edge.

Those who have gone before have left signposts: teachings and writings that instruct us in ways that awaken, that train the capacity to remember, that enable us to hold ourselves correctly as we move toward the light.

There is a human tendency to overlook our own obstacles, to ignore them or deny their existence even when we have seen them clearly. Therefore, it is difficult for us to achieve and sustain spiritual clarity without someone other than ourselves leading us beyond our own ignorance.

Systems, rules, practices, and stories embody much of the accumulated wisdom of those who have come before. Even though these resources are available, and have been proven to be invaluable, we all seem to have an endless capacity for deflecting the deepest truths, stepping carefully to one side or the other in order to avoid true self-recognition. However much we can learn on our own, and "be there" for one another as friends, lovers, and companions along the way, without guidance we are still likely to stumble as we try to make it along that sword's edge. Therefore, among Sufis, it is understood that at some point in your development you will need to work with a living teacher.

A teacher serves students, not by holding their hands and walking them across a chasm, but by supporting the rediscovery of that part of ourselves that knows where to put our feet. By helping us to reconnect with our own inner wisdom, the teacher empowers and enables us to continue the pilgrimage back to ourselves.

⌒

A donkey with a load of holy books is still a donkey.

Traditional

For every sin but the killing of Time there is forgiveness.

Traditional

Why lock up the stable after the horses are stolen? What is the use? You enjoyed the world until you became old and infirm. Now you say the world is unreal. Now you say you will find God—what is the use?

Oral teaching

If saying Ram [God] gave liberation
saying candy made your mouth sweet,
saying fire burned your feet,
saying water quenched your thirst,

saying food banished hunger,
the whole world would be free.

Kabir

Each faculty of ours delights in that for which it was created:
lust delights in accomplishing desire, anger in taking vengeance,
the eye in seeing beautiful objects, and the ear in hearing har-
monious sounds. The highest function of the soul is the perception of truth.

al-Ghazzali

Some say, "The Law tells us to abstain from anger, lust, and
hypocrisy. This is plainly impossible, for we are created with
those qualities inherent in us. You might as well tell us to make
black white." People ignore the fact that the law does not tell us
to uproot these passions but to restrain them within due limits
so that, by avoiding the great sins, we may obtain forgiveness of
the smaller ones. Even the Prophet of God said, "I am a man like
you, and get angry like others." In the Koran it is written, "God
loves those who swallow down their anger."

al-Ghazzali

When you commit a sin but do not carry the pleasure of it with
you, that is repentance. There is not so much harm in the act of
sinning as in the desire and thought of it: the act is but momentary and passing, whereas the desire is continuous. It is one
thing when the body indulges in a pleasurable act for an hour
and an entirely different thing when the mind and heart chew
on it endlessly.

Bushanja

People count with self-satisfaction the number of times they
have recited the name of God on their prayer beads, but they

keep no beads for reckoning the number of idle words they speak. Caliph Omar said, "Weigh well your words and deeds before they are weighed at the last judgment."

al-Ghazzali

Obligatory charity for the sake of God is due from every single part of your body, even from every root of your hair. In fact, charity is due for every instant of your life.

Charity of the eye means looking with consideration and averting your gaze from desires and things similar to them.

Charity of the ear means listening to the best of sounds, such as wisdom, the Koran, and the benefits of faith contained in warnings and good counsel, and by avoiding lies, slander, and similar things.

Charity of tongue means to give good advice, to awaken those who are heedless, and to give abundant glorification and remembrance and other, similar things.

Charity of hand means spending money on others, to be generous with God's blessing to you, to use your hand to write down knowledge and information by means of which others will benefit in obedience to God, and to restrain your hand from evil.

Charity of the foot means to hasten to carry one's duty to God by visiting virtuous people, attending assemblies of remembrance, putting things right between people, maintaining ties of kinship, engaging in *jihad* [inner struggle], and doing things that will make your heart sound and your faith correct.

al-Sadiq

A friend asked Nasruddin, "Why do you have a book tied to your leg?"

"So I won't lose it," replied Nasruddin.

"But you can't read it when it's tied to your leg."

"I can't read it if I lose it either."

Jeanette Berson

The roots of conduct have four aspects: conduct with God, conduct with self, conduct with people, and conduct with this world. Each of these aspects is based on seven principles. There are seven principles of conduct with God: giving God His due, keeping His limits, being thankful for His gift, being content with His decree, being patient with His trials, glorifying His sanctity, and yearning for Him.

The seven principles of conduct with self are reducing fear, striving, enduring harm, embracing spiritual discipline, seeking truthfulness and sincerity, withdrawing the self from what it loves, and binding it in poverty.

The seven principles of conduct with people are forbearance, forgiveness, humility, generosity, compassion, good counsel, justice and fairness.

The seven principles of conduct with this world are being content with what is at hand, preferring what is available to what is not, abandoning the quest for the elusive, hating over-abundance, choosing abstinence, knowing the evils of this world and abandoning any desire for them, and negating its dominance.

al-Sadiq

If someone remarks, "What an excellent man you are!" and this pleases you more than his saying, "What a bad man you are!" know that you are still a bad man.

Sufyan al-Thawri

A man said to Junaid, "True companions are scarce in these times. Where am I to find a companion in God?"

Junaid replied, "If you want a companion to provide for you and to bear your burden, such are few and far between. However, if you want a companion in God whose burden you will carry and whose pain you will bear, then I have a multitude I can introduce you to."

al-Ghazzali

It is related that Muhammad al-Ghazzali once rebuked his younger brother, Ahmad, saying, "People of every social rank, from every land, come to this city to perform prayer behind me, considering this good for their well-being in this world and a provision for their lives hereafter. Yet you, even though you are my brother and live close to me, refuse to say prayers behind me." Ahmad replied, "If you stand to lead prayers and struggle your utmost to say them in the full sense of the word, I will never turn away from following you."

At noon, Muhammad al-Ghazzali stood up to perform the prayers. Halfway through, Ahmad broke off, moved away, and continued his prayers in a different corner of the mosque.

After the imam completed his prayers, he came over to Ahmad and criticized him for his actions. Ahmad answered, "We were faithful to our promise. We followed you until you went to the stable to give water to our camel. We weren't able to continue our prayers after that because we lacked an imam to lead us."

With affection and friendship, Muhammad replied, "Glory be to God! He indeed has a group of His friends who are 'spies of our hearts.' My brother spoke truly, for it passed through my mind as I was delivering the prayer that I'd forgotten to give water to my camel."

Ahmad al-Ghazzali

On the Day of Judgment the Lord shall ask the learned men, "What did you do with the knowledge and the learning I conferred on you?" They will reply, "We spent it in Your way." The Lord shall say, "You are liars." And the angels shall also repeat the same charge. The Lord shall further say, "You spent it in earning applause, in passing for learned men and seeking praise of the people." Then the Lord shall ask the rich men, "I gave you wealth. What did you do with it?" They will say, "We gifted the riches in Your way." Then the Lord and the angels will say, "You are liars, you spent it so that people may call you very charitable." Then the Lord shall summon those who gave away their lives in the Holy Wars. They will be asked, "How did you spend your life I gave you?" They will reply, "We sacrificed it in Your Path." The Lord and the angels will call them liars and say, "You gave away your lives that people might call you brave and style you martyrs."

al-Ghazzali

One day the Prophet Abraham invited a person to dinner, but when he learned that he was an infidel he canceled the invitation and turned him out. Immediately the Divine Voice reprimanded him, saying, "You did not give him food for a day even because he belonged to a different religion, yet for the last seventy years I am feeding him in spite of his heresy. Had you fed him for one night, you would not have become poor on that account."

al-Ghazzali

A man of piety was following Christ. A thief seeing this thought to himself, "If I sit in the company of the pious one, perhaps God may for his sake forgive me." Prompted by humility in his heart, the thief started condemning himself for the impious life he had led. He considered himself unfit to sit by the side of such a saint. On the other hand, the pious man, seeing the thief seated by his side, reprimanded him lest his shadow corrupt him. Immediately Christ heard the Divine Voice say, "Tell the pious one and the thief that I have washed clean the scrolls of both. The virtues of the pious and the sins of the thief are washed clean. Now they must start life again. The virtues of the pious are washed away because of his pride, and the sins of the thief are washed away because of his humility and repentance."

al-Ghazzali

Arrogance and conceit in a person may be recognized by three signs:

1. When alone does he feel gloomy, and in company feel happy?
2. When people praise him, does he perform more worship?
3. When they speak badly of him, does he perform very little worship?

al-Ghazzali

One day Dhu-l-Nun reached a canal, where he performed his ablutions. He saw a beautiful palace situated close to the bank of the canal, on the balcony of which stood a very beautiful woman. Dhu-l-Nun asked her to speak to him.

She said, "When I saw you at a distance, I felt you were a madman; when you came closer, I saw you were a learned man; when you came closer still I considered you to be an enlightened soul. But now you have spoken to me I consider you none of these." Dhu-l-Nun asked her why she felt so. She replied, "If you were mad, you would not perform ablutions; if you were learned, you would not look at me; if you were enlightened, you would cast your glance at God and none besides." Saying this, she disappeared.

Attar

CHAPTER 4

The Lower Self

Sufism is concerned with the ways of following a spiritual path and with what gets us off track. There is an element in us, the nafs, *that tends to leads us astray. This Arabic term is sometimes translated "ego" or "self." Other meanings of* nafs *include "essence" and "breath."*

In Sufism, the term nafs *is generally used in the sense of "that which incites to wrongdoing." This includes our egotism and selfishness, our greed and unending desire for more things, our conceit and arrogance. Perhaps the best translation for this part of us is the "lower self."*

The lower self is not so much a thing as a process created by the interaction of the soul and the body. Body and soul are pure and blameless in themselves. However, when our soul becomes embodied, we tend to forget our soul-nature; we become attached to this world and develop such qualities as greed, lust, and pride.

On the spiritual path and in life in general, we all struggle to do those things we clearly know are best for ourselves and others. We often struggle even harder to avoid those actions we know are wrong or harmful.

Why the struggle? If we were of a single mind, there would be no struggle. But our minds are split. Even when we are convinced of what is right, our lower self tries to get us to do the opposite. Even when we see clearly, our lower self leads us to forget.

How the lower self operates, how to understand it, and how to work with it is vital for our soul's remembering. If we use it to work on ourselves, this material is precious beyond price.

⤻

The lower self always wants people to obey moral precepts only as *it* expounds them, to love it more than anything else. The lower self wants others to fear it in all situations, clinging to hope in its mercy, in the same way that God demands these things from His devotees.

Kashani

Happy are those who find fault with themselves instead of finding fault with others.

Muhammad

The lower self likes praise. It continually enjoins a person to put on pretensions, so that people will compliment it. Indeed, there are many worshipers and ascetics who are thus controlled by the lower self.

Qushayri

One of the latent vices and secret maladies of the lower self is its love of praise. Whoever imbibes a draught of it will try and move the seven heavens and seven sublunar realms for the flutter of an eyelash.

Qushayri

The lower self is like a flame both in its display of beauty and in its hidden potential for destruction; though its color is attractive, it burns.

Bakharzi

I saw my lower self in the form of a rat. I asked, "Who are you?" It replied, "I am the destruction of the heedless, for I incite them to wickedness. I am the salvation of the friends-of-God, for if it were not for me, they would be proud of their purity and their actions. When they see me in themselves, all their pride disappears."

Hujwiri

In most situations, the outward aspect of the lower self differs from the inward. It praises people in their presence, feigning honesty to their face, while in their absence it does the opposite.

Kashani

If a palace does not have a garbage pit next to it, it is incomplete. There must be a garbage pit next to a lofty palace so that all the refuse and filth that gather in the palace can be thrown there. In the same way, whenever God formed a heart by means of the light of purity, He placed this impure soul [the lower self] next to it as a dustbin. This black spot of "ignorance" flies on the same wings as the jewel of purity. There needs to be a bit of corruption so that purity can be built upon it. A straight arrow needs a crooked bow. O heart, you be like a straight arrow! O soul, you take the shape of a crooked bow!

When a peacock spreads out all its feathers, it gains a different joy from each feather. But as soon as it looks down at its own feet, it becomes embarrassed. That black spot of ignorance is the peacock's foot that always stays with you.

Samani

The lower self is obsessed with presenting itself in ways that gain the good opinion of others. This results in increase of possessions and pride in them, as well as arrogance, self-importance, and contempt. It avoids or ignores whatever people disapprove of, even though these things might please God.

Kashani

However much the lower self makes a show of virtue and attempts to conceal vice, the latter will be hidden only from the shortsighted and the naive, never from those with insight. It is like a hideous old hag who bedecks herself in fancy, dazzling clothes.

Kashani

The lower self is constantly preoccupied with the virtues of its attributes, contemplating its states with contentment and reverence. It considers important the least thing it has done for anyone, remembering it for years afterward, being overwhelmed by its own kindness. Yet however great the favors others do for it, it places no importance on them, forgetting them quickly.

Kashani

Whatever possessions and objects of its desires the lower self may obtain, it hangs on to them, refusing to let them go out of greed for more, or out of fear of poverty and need.

Rumi

A dervish was praying silently. A wealthy merchant, observing the dervish's devotion and sincerity, was deeply touched by him. The merchant offered the dervish a bag of gold. "I know that you will use the money for God's sake. Please take it."

"Just a moment." the dervish replied. "I'm not sure if it is lawful for me to take your money. Are you a wealthy man? Do you have more money at home?"

"Oh yes. I have at least one thousand gold pieces at home," claimed the merchant proudly.

"Do you want a thousand gold pieces more?" asked the dervish.

"Why yes, of course. Every day I work hard to earn more money."

"And do you wish for yet a thousand gold pieces more beyond that?"

"Certainly. Every day I pray that I may earn more and more money."

The dervish pushed the bag of gold back to the merchant. "I am sorry, but I cannot take your gold," he said. "A wealthy man cannot take money from a beggar."

"How can you call yourself a wealthy man and me a beggar?" the merchant spluttered.

The dervish replied, "I am a wealthy man because I am content with whatever God sends me. You are a beggar, because no matter how much you possess, you are always dissatisfied, and always begging God for more."

Sheikh Muzaffer

The lower self does not want anyone to receive anything from anybody else, and if it is aware of someone receiving a special boon, it seeks to destroy it.

Rumi

The lower self is continually subject to notions and whims, both in word and deed; it sticks with nothing and completes no project, only wanting to finish everything quickly. Its movements are arbitrary and unreliable; it is in a hurry to fulfill its desires, acting precipitously. Certain sages have likened it, in its fickleness, to a ball rolling giddily down a slope.

The lower self soon wearies of things. If, by any chance, the lower self should succeed in attaining what it wants, it will still not be satisfied. The lower self lacks stability.

Kashani

A so-called dragon hunter went to the mountains to trap a dragon. He searched the mountains and finally discovered the frozen body of a great dragon in a cave high up one of the tallest peaks. The man brought the body to Baghdad. He claimed he slew the dragon single-handed and exhibited it on the bank of the river. Hundreds of people came to see the dragon. The warmth of the Baghdad sun gradually warmed the dragon's body, and it began to stir, coming slowly out of its winter sleep. The people screamed and stampeded, and many were killed. The dragon hunter was frozen in fear, and the dragon ate him in a single gulp.

Your lower self is that dragon, a savage, bloody tyrant.
It is not dead, merely frozen.
Keep your dragon in the snow of self-discipline.
Do not transport it to the sunshine of Baghdad.
Let that dragon of yours remain dormant.
Should it be released, it will devour you.

Rumi

The lower self is so organized that it cannot be gotten rid of without the help of God.

Traditional

If you succeed in preventing the shadow of your lower self from falling on you, other people will gladly live under your shadow.

Traditional

As long as your lower self rules your heart, you will never lose your love of this world.

Traditional

The lower self prevents you from remembering God.

Traditional

If you treat your lower self with affection, you will never be saved from it.

Traditional

Those who are dead to their lower selves are alive with God.

Traditional

Those who are controlled by the lower self must serve it; those who control the lower self serve others.

Traditional

One way to train the lower self is to resist its desires. However, if we wish to resist, we know that we must not resist by opposing or suppressing it; for when we do, it will rear up somewhere else, seeking gratification of its desires.

Traditional

Continuous attention to God [remembrance] produces the gradual transmutation of the attributes of the lower self into the Attributes of God.

Nurbakhsh

The lower self is like a thief who sneaks into your house at night to steal whatever is valuable and worthwhile. You cannot fight this thief directly, because it will mirror whatever force you bring against it. If you have a gun, the thief will also have a gun. If you have a knife, the thief will have a knife as well. To struggle with the thief is to invite disaster. So, what can you do?

The only practical solution is to turn on the light. The thief, who is a coward at heart, will then run out. How do we turn on the light? Through the practice of remembrance, awareness, and heedfulness.

Sheikh Tosun Bayrak

CHAPTER 5

The World, Mirror of the Divine

There are two approaches to the world in almost every tradition. One is that heaven is separate from this world, accessible only after death. The other is that heaven (and hell) are here right now.

The Sufis say that this world can be heaven—when we love and bless one another, serve one another, and become the instruments for one another's inner growth and salvation. This world can also be a hell—in which we experience pain, betrayal, loss of love, and lack of caring.

Both aspects of the world are part of the divine order. This world is a place to taste the nectar of paradise and also to feel the coals of hell.

Some mystics in virtually all traditions reject the world, seeing it as a distraction or worse. They see the world as directly opposed to the search for God and the pursuit of spiritual growth. For the Sufis, God is found in the world; this world does not stand between us and God unless we put it there. Everything in this world can remind us of God.

All the world's beauty reminds us of the supreme Artist. The love found all around us—between parents and children, between lovers—is a sign of the Beloved.

A Bedouin was once asked how he could believe so strongly in a God he could not see. The man replied, "If you see the tracks of a camel in the desert, do you have to wait to see the camel itself before believing it exists?"

This world is our mirror. It mirrors our faults and failings as well as the Divine within each of us. As one sheikh has said, "Every rose is the reflection of a smile or a kind word, and every thorn the result of an unkind word or action."

The task for the Sufi is to polish the mirror of oneself so that one can catch the reflection of heaven during life—unmisted, undistorted, and in all its glory.

⏝

When you see beauty and perfection in this world, it is nothing but a sign of Him. A beautiful creature is merely a single blossom from the vast garden of God. But remember that a picture fades, a flower dies, and the reflection in the mirror is eclipsed by the real Light. It is God who is real and remains so forever. So, why waste your time over something that is here today and gone tomorrow? Go directly to the Source without delay.

Jami

Every form that you see has its original in the divine world. If the form passes away, it is of no consequence, because its original was from eternity. Be not grieved that every form that you see, every mystical saying that you have heard will pass away. The fountainhead is always bringing forth water. Since neither ceases, why should you complain? Consider this spirit as a fountain; rivers flow from it. Put regret out of your thoughts, and keep on drinking from the rivulet. Do not be afraid. The water is limitless.

When you came into the world of created beings, a ladder was set before you, so that you might pass out of it. At first you were inanimate, then you became a plant; afterward you were changed into an animal. At last you became human, possessed of knowledge, intelligence, and faith. Next, you will become an angel. Then you will have finished with this world, and your place will be in the heavens. Be changed also from the station of an angel. Pass into that mighty deep, so that the one drop, which is yourself, may become a sea.

Rumi

Habib had one cloak that he used to wear both summer and winter. One day, when he went out of his house to make ablutions, he left his cloak behind on the road. Hasan al-Basri came by and saw Habib's cloak lying in the middle of the road. He thought to himself, "Habib has left his cloak; may God forbid that someone take it." Hasan stood there and watched over the coat until Habib returned. When Habib arrived, he greeted Hasan and said, "O Imam of the Muslims, what are you doing standing there?" Hasan exclaimed, "Don't you know that your coat should not be left here? Someone might take it. Tell me, in whom were you trusting leaving it here?" Habib replied, "In He who appointed you to watch over it."

al-'Ajami

Bahlul, the wise fool, happened to meet the caliph Harun al-Rashid. "Where are you coming from like this, Bahlul?" the ruler asked him.

"From Hell," was the prompt reply.

"What were you doing there?"

Bahlul explained, "Fire was needed, Sire, so I thought of going to Hell to ask if they could spare a little. But the fellow in charge there said, 'We have no fire here.' Of course I asked him, 'How come? Isn't Hell the place of fire?' He answered, 'I tell you, there really is no fire down here. Everybody brings his own fire with him when he comes.'"

Sheikh Muzaffer

All that we behold and perceive by our senses bears undeniable witness to the existence of God—the stone and the clod, the plants and the trees, the living creatures, the heavens and the earth and the stars, the dry land and the ocean, the fire and the air, substance and accident. Indeed, we ourselves are the chief witnesses to Him. But just as the bat sees only at night and cannot see in the daytime because of the weakness of its sight, which is dazzled by the full light of the sun, so also the human mind is too weak to behold the full glory of the Divine Majesty.

al-Ghazzali

The Chinese said to the king, "We are the better artists," and the Greeks rejoined, "We have more skill than you and a greater sense of beauty." The king gave each a room, with doors opposite each other.

The Chinese asked the king for a hundred different colors, gold and silver, and gems. The Greeks asked only for polish and polishing cloths and shut themselves in and polished continuously.

When the Chinese finished their work, the king entered and looked at the pictures they had painted. He was awestruck by their beauty. Then, the Greeks raised the curtain that was between the rooms. The reflection of the paintings fell upon the polished walls, and all that the king had seen before seemed even more lovely there.

The Greeks are the Sufis who have purified their hearts. The pure heart is a spotless mirror that receives innumerable images.

The pure have left behind fragrance and color; each moment
they see Beauty without hindrance.

Rumi

When you are separate from the Kaaba [the holy shrine in
Mecca, the place all Muslims turn toward when they pray], it is
all right to turn toward it, but those who are *in* it can turn toward any direction they wish.

Bayazid Bistami

One day I was carrying something disgusting in my hands. My
companions imagined I was carrying it with the intention of
mortifying my soul because in their eyes I was much too lofty to
stoop to carrying such a thing. They told this to my sheikh, who
then questioned me. I replied that it was simply that I saw that
God did not disdain to create such a thing. How then was I to
disdain to carry it?

Ibn al-'Imad

Sufism is good character, so anyone who improves your character has improved your Sufism also.

al-Kattani

One day, the caliph Omar met a group of people who were sitting around doing nothing. He asked them who they were. "We
are of those who put their affairs in the hands of God, and we
trust in God." they replied.

"Indeed you do not!" he retorted. "You are nothing but free-
loaders, parasites upon other people's efforts! Someone who
truly trusts in God first plants seed in the belly of this earth,
then puts his affairs in the hand of God, the Sustainer!"

Ibn 'Arabi

God created the souls four thousand years before He created
their bodies. The souls were bathed and nourished in the divine
light. Those who live in fellowship and harmony in this world
must have been on terms of intimacy there. Here they have
friendship with one another and are called the Sufis, the "friends
of God." They are in that state because they love one another for
the sake of God.

Abu Sa'id

One day someone asked the prophet Muhammad, "What was all
of this universe created for? How does it exist?" The Prophet answered, "I don't know the answer. I'll have to go and ask the
angel Gabriel." So he went and asked Gabriel, who answered, "I
don't know the answer to that, I'll have to go ask Allah." So
Gabriel asked Allah, and then returned and said, "Allah said, 'I
have created the skies and heavens simply as a beautiful sight
and an entertainment for you, and to create wonder and awe of
My majesty and power. I want the blinking stars to uplift and
delight you and cause you to marvel at my creation.'"

Moinuddin

If I appear to be remiss in gratitude and appreciation and offering thanks for the kindnesses and support you show me directly
and indirectly, this is not out of arrogance or indifference, or because I do not know what it behooves the recipient of a favor to
say and do. But I was aware of the purity of your faith, that you
do those things sincerely for the sake of God; so I leave it to God
to thank you Himself. If I were to concern myself with thanking
you and praising you, it would be as though some part of the reward that God is going to give you had already been paid.

Rumi

CHAPTER 6

Wisdom

What is wisdom? The prophet Muhammad defined wisdom as follows:

> *Do what you should do when you should do it.*
> *Refuse to do what you should not do;*
> *And, when it is not clear, wait until you are sure.*

We all like to think that we are wise. And that is certainly one reason we keep making so many foolish mistakes. To pretend to wisdom is to ignore the reality of our own shortcomings. How can we learn from our mistakes until we are wise enough to look at them clearly? Humility and self-awareness are among the prerequisites to wisdom.

Action is the final essential component of wisdom. Knowledge not acted upon is merely a collection of facts. As the Sufis are fond of saying, "A donkey with a load of books is still a donkey." But when we act on our knowledge, we open ourselves up to wisdom. Sheikh Safer, the current head of one of the major Sufi orders, has said, "I don't know very much about Sufism, but what I do know I have learned with love and I have practiced that for over forty years."

If we listen closely to the words of the wise, and we act on them, perhaps we ourselves will one day be counted among their ranks. Then, our own words will serve to guide others.

⟳

A great king summoned his wise men. He ordered them, "Create for me a saying that will stabilize my inner state. When I am unhappy it will bring me joy, and when I am happy it will remind me of sadness. It cannot be too long, as I want to keep it with me always."

The wise men consulted and contemplated deeply the king's command. Finally, they returned to the king bearing a small box. In it there was a ring, and inside the ring was inscribed the following words: "This too shall pass."

Attar

Act as if there were no one on earth but you and no one in Heaven but God.

al-Antaki

True knowledge comes through the light of certainty, by which God enlightens the heart. Then, you will behold the things of the spiritual world, and by the power of that light all the veils between you and that world will be removed.

al-Antaki

If you wish for a pearl
you must leave the desert
and wander by the sea;
and even if you never find
the gleaming pearl, at least
you won't have failed to reach the water.

Sama'i

A wise student asked, "Teach me how to learn and what to study." An even wiser student prayed, "Let me sincerely wish to learn how to learn."

Ali Ramitani

All wisdom can be stated in two lines:
What is done for you—allow it to be done.
What you must do yourself—make sure you do it.

Khawwas

Speech is priceless
if you speak with knowledge.
Weigh it in the scales of the heart
before it comes from the mouth.

Kabir

You may follow one stream. Know that it leads to the Ocean, but do not mistake the stream for the Ocean.

Jan-Fishan

He who knows not, and knows not that he knows not, is a
      fool—shun him.
He who knows not, and knows that he knows not, is a
      child—teach him.
He who knows, and knows not that he knows, is asleep—
      wake him.
But he who knows, and knows that he knows, is a wise
      man—follow him.

Traditional

Nasruddin addressed a crowd saying, "People, do you want knowledge without difficulties, truth without falsehood, attainment without effort, progress without sacrifice?"

Everyone shouted, "Yes, yes!"

"Wonderful!" said Nasruddin. "I do too, and if I ever discover how to do it, I will be delighted to tell you."

Traditional

A sheikh said, "If you wish to become a saint, change your character into the character of children." "Why?" he was asked. "Children have five qualities," he answered, "and if adults had these same qualities, they would attain the rank of saints."

1. They do not worry about their daily bread.
2. When they fall sick, they do not complain night and day about their misfortune.
3. Whatever food they have, they share.
4. When they fight or quarrel, they do not keep grudges in their hearts, but make up quickly.
5. The slightest threat makes them frightened and brings tears to their eyes.

al-Ghazzali

Asking good questions is half of learning.

Muhammad

Once Ibrahim Adhem saw a stone on which was written, "Turn me over and read." On the other side he read, "You do not practice what you know. Why, then, do you seek what you know not?"

Hujwiri

There was a great sheikh whose fame spread until even the sultan heard of him. The sultan began coming to visit the sheikh's lodge every Thursday evening to hear the sheikh teach and to participate in the prayers and chanting of God's Names.

After some time, the sultan said to the sheikh, "I really love you and your teachings. Ask me for whatever you want. If it is in my power, I will grant it."

The sheikh replied, "I do have one request of you, my sultan. Please do not come back."

"You see, before you came to us, my dervishes would chant and pray to God, seeking only God's favor and blessings. Since you have been coming here, they have been trying to please you. They still covet the power and riches you represent. So I must ask you not to come back, because we are not developed enough to support your presence."

Sheikh Muzaffer

Whoever goes out in search of knowledge is on the path of God until they return.

Muhammad

People of knowledge are the inheritors of the Prophets.

Muhammad

Possessors of knowledge and seekers of knowledge are the only two groups of any use to humanity.

Muhammad

He who is intimate with worldly wealth will find his intellect destroyed; he who is intimate with people will become lonely; he who is intimate with work will be preoccupied; and he who is intimate with God will attain union.

Shibli

People have spoken much concerning poverty and wealth and have chosen one or the other for themselves, but I choose whichever state God chooses for me and keeps me in. If God keeps me rich, I will not be forgetful, and if God wishes me to be poor, I will not be covetous and rebellious. Wealth and poverty are divine gifts. Wealth is corrupted by forgetfulness, poverty by greed.

Qushayri

The Almighty created the angels and conferred reason
upon them, and He created the beasts and conferred passion
upon them, and He created man and conferred reason and
passion both upon him. He whose reason prevails over his passion is higher than the angels, and he whose passion prevails
over his reason is lower than the beasts.

Muhammad

If a man gives up quarreling when he is in the wrong, a house
will be built for him in Paradise. But if a man gives up a conflict
even when he is in the right, a house will be built for him in the
loftiest part of Paradise.

Muhammad

Ali asked the Prophet, "What action can I take that is not totally
lost and worthless?"

The Prophet answered, "Seek truth. You will find it in yourself; therefore, know yourself. Seek the company of the wise,
who know. Agree with what they say, for one understands only
that with which one agrees. Be sincere in what you say—a single
tongue should not speak two different words. No deceit or fraud
should enter into your thoughts. Do not belittle anyone or anything, for everyone and everything in its inner being wishes for
the same thing.

"Do not touch anything that is not yours. Avoid crowded
places; even in such places, try to be with yourself, for that is the
place where the truth is manifested. That is where the truth is."

Ibn 'Arabi

Guard your heart from heedlessness, protect your lower self
from desires, guard your intellect from ignorance, and you will
be admitted into the company of the vigilant. It is a duty for
everyone to seek knowledge; that is, knowledge of yourself.

al-Sadiq

Wisdom is like the rain. Its source is unlimited, but it comes down according to the season. Grocers put sugar in a bag, but their supply of sugar is not the amount in the bag. When you come to a grocer, he has sugar in abundance. But he sees how much money you have brought and gives accordingly.

Your currency on this Path is resolution and faith, and you are taught according to your resolution and faith. When you come seeking sugar, they examine your bag to see what its capacity is; then they measure out accordingly.

Rumi

A sultan was riding through the country surrounded by courtiers and soldiers. Everybody bowed as the sultan passed, except for a single dervish.

The sultan halted his procession and had the dervish brought to him. He demanded to know why the man did not bow to him.

The dervish replied, "Let all these people bow to you. They all want what you have—money, power, rank. Thank God these things mean nothing to me." Then he added, "Furthermore, a free man should not bow down to a slave."

"What do you mean?" the sultan cried.

"You are a slave to anger and greed," the dervish said calmly, looking the sultan full in the face. "I have made them my servants and become a free man."

Recognizing the truth of what he heard, the sultan bowed to the dervish.

Sheikh Muzaffer

One day, Jesus was walking in the desert with a group of self-seeking people. They begged him to tell them the Secret Name by which he restored the dead to living. Jesus said, "If I tell you, you will abuse its power." The people promised they would use the knowledge wisely and begged him again.

"You do not know what you ask," he said, but he told them the Word.

Soon after, the group was walking in a deserted place when they saw a heap of whitened bones. "Let us try out the Word," they said to each other, and they did.

The moment the Word was pronounced, the bones became clothed with flesh and transformed into a wild beast, which tore them to shreds.

Rumi

The drowning man is not troubled by rain.

Traditional

As he was walking, Moses heard a shepherd praying to God, offering to comb God's hair, wash God's robe, and kiss His hand. Moses scolded the shepherd for his blasphemy. That night God appeared to Moses and admonished him. "You have driven away a worshiper from his worship. In his sincere, simple way, that shepherd was much closer to me than most scholars and ascetics."

Rumi

One day, Rabia was seen running, carrying fire in one hand and water in the other. They asked her the meaning of her action and where she was going. She replied, "I am going to light a fire in Paradise and pour water on Hell, so that both veils (hindrances to the true vision of God) completely disappear."

Rabia

O my Lord, if I worship You from fear of Hell, burn me in Hell; and if I worship You from hope of Paradise, exclude me from Paradise. But if I worship You for Your own sake, do not withhold from me Your Eternal Beauty.

Rabia

CHAPTER 7

Hadith, the Words of the Prophet

Most Sufis have grown up with the words of the Prophet. They are an integral part of the folk wisdom and the spiritual tradition in which Sufism has developed and flourished. Many of these sayings seem as if they were written just yesterday to deal with today's problems and issues. They provide another reminder that real wisdom is timeless.

These sayings are known as hadith, *or the traditions of the Prophet. They were originally taken from records made during Muhammad's lifetime and immediately after. Classic* hadith *collections include listings of the witnesses who vouched for the veracity of each saying. The stricter collections include only sayings verified by at least three men or women of honest reputation and impeccable character.*

Many different collections of wisdom sayings have been compiled. It is considered a blessing to pass down timeless wisdom and true guidance to others.

Divine breezes from your Lord waft through the days of your life. Listen! Be aware of them.

Would you have me tell you about actions that are better than fasting, prayer, and charity? Bring goodness and high principles between people.

When God desires goodness for a human being, he will discover a voice of wisdom within his own being that shall lead him to the road of goodness.

Success will follow patience, opening will follow hardship, and ease will follow difficulties.

Wish for others whatever you wish for yourself.

Belief [faith] is the knowledge of the heart, the words of the tongue, and the actions of the body.

If your words are truthful, if you are good-tempered, if you are moderate in taking food, and if you are trustworthy, then you are rich and should not regret the possessions that you may not have. These four qualities are enough possessions and wealth for a wise person.

The signs of misfortune lie in four conditions: eyes that have never experienced tears, a heart that is cruel and hard, long chains of desires that never end, and wishing for an extremely prolonged life.

One who can control himself when in anger, in passion, in fear, and in attraction is safe from the hands of the devil and the fires of hell.

Have pity upon three groups of people: a dear person who has lost his loved ones, a rich person who has lost his wealth, and a learned one who is trapped among the ignorant.

Have mercy on people so you may receive mercy; forgive people so you may be forgiven.

I do not worry about the things that you do not know, but I am cautious in appraising how you apply what you do know.

Avoid three qualities: jealousy, greed, and arrogance.
Be pious in your inner self and outer life: if you have behaved badly, then do a good deed right away; do not ask anything from anyone; do not borrow anything from anyone; and do not make yourself a judge between two people.

The first stage of worship is silence.

Do not commit yourself to lengthy discussions of religion— such talk only succeeds in making religion a complex and confused matter. God has made religion easy and simple.

If you want to live more freely, borrow less.

Avoid greed, for greed in itself is poverty.

The most ignorant among you is the one who does not learn from the changes in the world.
   The richest among you is the one who is not entrapped by greed.

There is an organ in the body that, if it is righteous, ensures that the whole system will be righteous; and if it is corrupt, the whole body will become corrupt. This organ is the heart.

The strongest among you is the one who controls his anger.

Jealousy destroys good acts just as fire burns wood; charity consumes sin the same way that water quenches fire.

God despises the tyrannical wealthy, the ignorant elderly, and the selfish poor.

Follow truthfulness even if you think it may harm you, for truthfulness never harms but instead saves. Do not lie even if you think it will protect you. Lying never protects, it only destroys.

Protect and honor the earth, for the earth is like your mother.

Value the worth of five things before they are replaced by the other five conditions: value your youthfulness before old age arrives, value health before sickness strikes, value your wealth before you become needy, value peacefulness before hardship comes, and value life before death arrives.

Generations before you were destroyed because they declined to punish the powerful thieves yet were relentless in punishing the small pickpockets.

The cure of ignorance is to ask and learn.

Avoid noise, excessive talking, too many questions, too many answers, and wasting your wealth.

The old are our bounty, and whoever is not compassionate toward our elders and our youth, and whoever does not honor them, does not belong to my people.

Worship God as if you see Him, and remember that even if you see Him not, He still sees you.

There are those who believe that if they study the Koran, and so learn the words of the knowledge of religion, and then go to kings and princes to seek favor from them, that they can keep safe their piety. It is not so. From a thorny tree you will get naught by thorns, and likewise you will get nothing from kings except sins to commit.

Avoid stubbornness, for it begins in ignorance and ends in regret.

Be kind to people whether they deserve your kindness or not. If your kindness reaches the deserving, good for you; if your kindness reaches the undeserving, take joy in your compassion.

Promise me six conditions so that I may promise you Paradise: be truthful, do not break your promises, return whatever you are given to safeguard, keep yourself from impure friendships, keep your eyes from unfair glances, and keep your hands from worthless actions.

Oh God, bring peacefulness among us, bring unity into our hearts; guide us to equilibrium, take us from darkness to light and away from ugliness; bless our ears, our eyes, our hearts, and our families; accept our repentance.

Moderate spending is half the earning; making friends with people is half the wisdom; and asking good questions is half the knowing.

God will not show mercy to him who does not show mercy to others.

The believer is a mirror to the believer.

Trust in God, but tie your camel's leg.

Envy consumes good deeds as fire consumes wood.

Happy are those whose own faults preoccupy them too much to think of the faults of others.

Heaven lies under the feet of mothers.

None of you truly believes until he wishes for his brother what he wishes for himself.

The person who repents is like one who has never sinned.

God exalts the humble and humbles the proud.

True wealth is not abundance in property but a generous heart.

Surely God does not judge you by appearance or property but by [the goodness of your] heart and deeds.

God was asked why creation came into being. "I was a hidden treasure. I longed to be known, so I created all of creation."

God is beautiful and loves beauty.

There are as many ways to God as there are created souls.

Wealth does not reside in the amount of one's property, but rather in one's own needlessness.

An hour of contemplation is better than a year of prayer.

For none of you will faith be rectified unless your hearts be
            made right,
nor will your hearts be rectified unless your tongues be made
            right,
nor will your tongues be rectified unless your actions be
            made right.

Two believers that lend support to each other are like a pair of hands that wash each other clean.

One who suffers oppression and forgives the oppressor is the most favored for aid from God.

Asceticism for the sake of the world brings relief to the body; asceticism for the sake of the hereafter brings relief to the heart; and turning one's face toward the Divine brings relief to the Spirit.

Whenever God loves a devotee, He subjects him to ordeals. Should he endure patiently, God singles him out; should he be content, God purifies him.

PART 3

Love and an Open Heart

CHAPTER 8

Spiritual Experience

There are times when the veils between us and God are thinned, times of rich and rewarding spiritual experience. The most profound spiritual experience might come to us at any time, anywhere. God has revealed, through the prophet Muhammad, "There are seventy thousand veils between you and Me, and there are no veils between Me and you."

Sometimes we feel God's presence directly. More often that presence manifests indirectly—as an opening of the heart, a burst of joy, an expansion of love, or feelings of deep compassion. We also may deeply experience God in sorrow, during times of loss as well as times of joy.

We have all had spiritual experiences. We have not always had the words for these experiences, so we may not have recognized them for what they were. A Gallup poll taken several years ago found that over 65 percent of Americans have had deeply meaningful, extraordinary experiences, experiences that have changed their lives in significant ways. We are all mystics, although we may use different terms for what holds life's mysteries and deepest meanings for each of us.

It may be that during times of spiritual experience, we are most truly ourselves. Our daily level of awareness can be seen as a severely limited sample of what we are truly capable of. Sufi teachers have written that our everyday, basic level of consciousness might be best described as a kind of "waking sleep." To wake up is to wake up to the Divine.

⇌

I died from minerality and became vegetable;
And from vegetativeness I died and became animal.
I died from animality and became human.
Then why fear disappearance through death?
Next time I shall die
Bring forth wings and feathers like angels;
After that, soaring higher than angels—
What you cannot imagine
I shall be that.

Rumi

For thirty years I sought God. But when I looked carefully I found that in reality God was the seeker and I the sought.

Bayazid Bistami

When you come upon the essence, do you still want the form? When you have drunk of the water of life, do you still need the glass to contain it?

Reshad Feild

We have placed in you a substance, a seeking, a yearning, and We are watching over it and won't let it be lost, but will bring it to its destined place.

Rumi

Say "God" just once and then stand fast, as every affliction rains down upon you! The Prophet said, "Wherever our religion goes, it doesn't come back without uprooting a person and sweeping his house clean and cleansing him." For this reason you have no peace, but rather pain. Being troubled means being emptied of the joys and the untroubled mood of initial ignorance.

Be patient and troubled. "Eating trouble" is an emptying-out. After the emptying, joy appears, a joy that knows no trouble, a rose that has no thorns, a wine that causes no hangovers.

Rumi

If in thirst you drink water from a cup, you see God in it. Those who are not in love with God will see only their own faces in it.

Rumi

Silence for the ordinary people is with their tongues, silence for the mystics is with their hearts, and silence for the lovers is with restraining the stray thoughts that come to their innermost beings.

Traditional

Lovers converse with people only as much as they need to. For the most part, they prefer to be alone and by themselves. for they yearn for intimate communion with the Beloved. They are constantly in meditation. They do not enjoy excessive conversation and always prefer not to talk. They do not understand conversation about anything other than God.

When they encounter misfortune, they do not grumble and complain. They know that misfortune comes from the Friend, and see the benefits contained in seeming misfortune. Divine Love has possessed them, and they have plunged lovingly into the fire of love. Going barefoot, bareheaded, and poorly clad does not worry them at all.

They hear no word but the words of God. They never cease from the remembrance of God. Everywhere they behold God's Beauty. Their aim is God alone, and their desire is God's good pleasure.

Sheikh Muzaffer

One day a man seated next to Hasan displayed a miracle by bringing out a live fish from a tumbler of water. Hasan placed his hand in a burning oven and brought out a live fish. The man challenged Hasan to jump in the fire with him to see who would survive. Hasan replied, "Miracle-mongering will not do. Let us drown ourselves in the ocean of nonexistence and come out cloaked with the garment of divine existence." The man was silent.

Attar

The sight of someone eating will not appease your hunger. The spiritual experiences of others cannot satisfy your yearning.

Traditional

Now, to those who lay claim to love I address these questions:

How often have you wiped away the tears of a lover weeping for love of God?

Have you yourself ever shed a single tear for love of God?

How many nights have you spent without sleep for love of God?

What sacrifices have you been able to bear for love of God?

Sheikh Muzaffer

The Sufi is pleased with all that God does in order that God may be pleased with all that he does.

Abu Sa'id

I hold you in my heart.
I rock and sing you to sleep.
You are everywhere in everyone,
the holy baby in all of us,
that plays there.

The beautiful one,
born when we love,
the glowing child.

You are the meaning that blooms in the heart.
                    Bawa Muhaiyaddeen

Happy is he who is able to escape from the lower self and feel
the gentle breeze of friendship. His heart is so full of the Beloved
that there is no longer room for anyone else. The Beloved flows
through his every vein and nerve. Every atom of his body is
filled with the Friend.

The true lovers can no longer perceive either the scent or the
color of their own selves. They have no interest in anything
other than the Beloved. Their heart is attached neither to throne
nor crown. Greed and lust have packed their bags and left their
street. If they speak, it is to the Friend. If they seek, it is from the
Friend. They no longer take themselves into account, and live
only for love. They leave the raw and turn to the ripe, abandoning completely the abode of the self.

                                        Jami

CHAPTER 9

Opening the Heart

When the eyes of the heart open, we can see the inner realities hidden behind the outer forms of this world. When the ears of the heart open, we can hear what is hidden behind words; we can hear truth.

Opening the heart means coming closer to God. God said, through Muhammad, "I who cannot be fit into universes upon universes, fit into the heart of the sincere believer." The heart is a temple that can house God. All hearts are temples, and to open our hearts is to allow in the divine presence.

The heart of hearts in each of us houses a spark of the Divine. This is the meaning of the biblical (and also Koranic) quote, "And God breathed the breath of life [ruach] into Adam." The primary meaning for the Hebrew word ruach is "spirit," so this sentence might be more accurately translated "And God breathed divine spirit into Adam." As our hearts open, we come more in touch with the wisdom, love, joy, and inspiration from the divine spark within.

All wisdom is already within us; all love is already within us, all joy. Yet they are hidden within us until the heart opens.

Dear friend,

Your heart is a polished mirror. You must wipe it clean of the veil of dust that has gathered upon it, because it is destined to reflect the light of divine secrets.

al-Ghazzali

Go you, sweep out the dwelling room of your heart, prepare it to be the home of the Beloved. When you go out, He will come in. Within you, when you are free from self, He will show His beauty.

Shabistari

There is a polish for everything that takes away rust; and the polish of the heart is *dhikr,* the invocation of God.

Muhammad

Oh heart, sit with someone
who knows the heart;
Go under the tree
which has fresh blossoms.

Rumi

Omar asked the Prophet what things were especially to be sought in the world. The Prophet answered, "A tongue occupied in the remembrance of God, a grateful heart, and a believing wife."

al-Ghazzali

Fasting is a way to save on food.
Vigil and prayer is a labor for old folks.
Pilgrimage is an occasion for tourism.
To distribute bread in alms is something for philanthropists.
Fall in love:
That is doing something!

Ansari

Truth has been planted in the center of your heart, entrusted to you by God for safekeeping. It becomes manifest with true repentance and with true effort. Its beauty shines on the surface when you remember God and do the *dhikr* [recitation of Divine Names]. At the first stage you recite the name of God with your tongue; then, when your heart becomes alive, you recite inwardly with the heart.

Abdul Qadir al-Jilani

There is a city in which you find everything that you desire— handsome people, pleasures, ornaments of every kind—all that the natural person craves for. However, you cannot find a single wise person there. Would that it were the very opposite!

That city is the human being. If there were a hundred thousand accomplishments there but not that essential element, the loving heart, it would be better for that city to be in ruins.

Rumi

Become a person of the heart
—or at least the devotee of one;
Or else, you will remain
like a donkey stuck in the mud.

If one has no heart,
one can gain no benefit;
In wretchedness, one
will be famous in the world.

Rumi

The heart of the believer is the sanctuary of God, and nothing but God is allowed access there.

Muhammad

The Sufis refer to a spiritual state as a "baby," because that baby is born in the heart and is reared and grows there. The heart, like a mother, gives birth, suckles, and rears the child of the heart. As worldly sciences are taught to children, the child of the heart is taught inner wisdom. As an ordinary child is not yet soiled with worldly sins, the child of the heart is pure, free from heedlessness, egotism, and doubt. The purity of a child appears often as physical beauty; in dreams, the purity of the heart's child appears in the shape of angels. We hope to enter Paradise as a reward for good deeds, but gifts of Paradise come here through the hands of the child of the heart.

Abdul Qadir al-Jilani

The heart is the treasury
in which God's mysteries are stored;
Seek the purpose of both the worlds
through the heart,
for that is the point of it.

Lahiji

The rational soul in man abounds in marvels, both of knowledge and power. By means of it we master arts and sciences, can pass in a flash from earth to heaven and back again, can map out the skies and measure the distances between the stars. By it also we can draw the fish from the sea and the birds from the air and can subdue to our service animals like the elephant, the camel, and the horse. Our five senses are like five doors opening on the external world; but, more wonderful than this, our heart has a window that opens on the unseen world of spirit.

In the state of sleep, when the avenues of the senses are closed, this window is opened, and we receive impressions from the unseen world and sometimes foreshadowings of the future. Our hearts are like a mirror that reflects what is pictured in the Tablet of Fate. But, even in sleep, thoughts of worldly things dull this mirror, so that the impressions it receives are not clear. After death, however, such thoughts vanish, and things are seen in their naked reality.

al-Ghazzali

God said, through the Prophet, "Man is my secret and I am his secret. The inner knowledge of the spiritual essence is a secret of My secrets. Only I put this into the heart of My good servant, and none may know his state other than Me."

Abdul Qadir al-Jilani

Remembering God is the cure for the heart.

Muhammad

It is a principle of beauty that a fair face cannot bear to remain hidden behind the curtain; it is incapable of modesty, and if you close the door on it, it will only appear at the window. As you yourself know, when a rare and wonderful idea arises in your mind, you become obsessed with it and have to express it in speech or writing.

Jami

The heart is the king and the limbs are its servants. Each limb functions according to the will and command of the heart, and the will of the heart comes from God

Only God is over the heart, and no one else can see what the heart contains. God alone places in the heart or removes from the heart whatever He wills. The heart is the place of God's Unity and the object of God's observation.

God watches over the hearts, for they are the containers of His most precious jewels and treasure stores of the true knowledge of Him.

al-Tirmidhi

CHAPTER 10

Contemplation and Knowledge

Robert Service, in his best-known poem, "The Shooting of Dan McGrew," draws a distinction between different kinds of hungers. There is

> *Hunger that's not of the belly kind, that's banished with*
> *bacon and beans,*
> *But the gnawing hunger of lonely men for a home and all*
> *that it means.*

So it is with knowledge as well. There is knowledge of the stuff of this world: batting averages, stock reports, car colors, breeds of dogs, and recipes. There is the knowledge of chemical reactions, the history of nations, and the postmodernist school of contemporary art. All of these are "of the belly kind," that is, bacon and beans. The other, the gnawing hunger of lonely men, is not appeased by information or facts. It comes from a different realm. When one is lifted out of the sleep of forgetfulness, one knows that there is something far beyond the food that satisfies intellectual hunger, that transcends the desire to know the ingredients in a loaf of bread or the number of fat grams in a serving of butter.

When all of earthly knowledge is forced through the sieve of contemplation, the few grains that remain are "the pure gold of Spiritual sustenance" that provides true nourishment. The rest is chaff and falls through to the ground below. Little of what we think we know intellectually can be used to bake Divine bread.

The poet laureate of the United States, Robert Hass, observing the mating of dragonflies, speaks of the "after-longing" that evolution has worked out in order to "suck the last juice of this world into the receiver body." The knowledge that arises from contemplation is that knowledge that whirls the earth about the sun, that raises and lowers the tides, that opens eyes and, eventually, for the devoted student, the heart.

Those whose desire to see is strong enough will discern the hand of the designer in the symmetrical pattern of the leaves, the paint strokes of the artist in the strata of the rocks, the blueprints of the engineer in the placement of the stars.

⇔

A group of people once commended a certain man in the presence of the Prophet, praising him excessively. Thereupon the Prophet said, "What kind of intellect does he have?" But they replied, saying, "We tell thee about his diligence in prayer and about the various good works he does, and you ask us about his intellect?" The Prophet answered and said, "The fool does more harm through his ignorance than do the wicked through their wickedness."

Muhammad

Ali and Hasan went out bear hunting. For four days they saw nothing. Each night they slept in a nearby village, pledging part of the bear's skin against the cost of their lodging. On the fifth day a huge bear appeared, and Ali said nervously to his friend, "I don't mind confessing that I'm afraid to take this bear." Hasan laughed, "Just leave it to me." So Ali scrambled like lightning up the nearest tree, and Hasan stood with his gun at the ready. The bear came lumbering on, and Hasan began to grow more and more scared. At length he raised his gun to his shoulder, but by now he was trembling so much that, before he could take proper aim, his gun went off and missed the target. Hasan, remembering that bears never touch a dead body, threw himself flat and held his breath. The bear came up, sniffed all around him and finally made off. Ali, who had been watching the whole affair from his tree, now came down and, congratulating Hasan on his escape, asked him, "What did the bear whisper in your ear?"

"Don't sell the bearskin before you have caught the bear."

Traditional

He who knows three things is saved from three things:

Who knows that the Creator made no mistakes at Creation is saved from petty fault finding.

Who knows that He made no favoritism in allotting fortune is saved from jealousy.

Who knows of what he is created is saved from pride.

Ansari

Loqman the philosopher, being asked from whom he had learned wisdom, replied, "From the blind, who do not take a step before trying the place."

Sam Lewis

Salih always taught his disciples, "Who knocks at the door of someone constantly, one day the door must be opened to him." Rabia one day heard it and said, "Salih, how long will you go on preaching thus, using the future tense, saying, 'will be opened'? Was the door ever closed?" Salih bowed in submission to her.

Attar

Hasan al-Basri asked, "al-'Ajami, how did you attain to such spiritual height?"

"By whitening the heart, by prayers and by not darkening papers by writing."

Attar

Once Hasan al-Basri went to Habib al-'Ajami at the time of evening prayers. Hasan heard al-'Ajami mispronounce a word during the prayer. He considered it improper to say his prayers with him, and therefore said them separately. During the night he dreamed the Lord spoke to him: "Hasan, if you had stood behind al-'Ajami and said your prayers, you would have earned Our pleasure, and that single prayer of yours would have borne thee greater benefit than all prayers taken together that you have offered in your lifetime. You found fault with his pronunciation but ignored the purity and excellence of his heart. Know it that We cherish a contrite heart much more than the correct pronunciation of words.

Attar

On my first journey I found a kind of knowledge acceptable to both the elect and the common folk, on the second, knowledge acceptable to the elect and not the common folk, and on the third, knowledge acceptable to neither the elect nor the common folk; thus I remained an outcast and alone.

The first kind of knowledge was repentance, which both the elect and the common folk accept, the second was trust in God and fellowship with Him and love, which the elect accept, and the third was the knowledge of reality, which is beyond the power of human learning and reason to attain, so men reject it.

Dhu-l-Nun

The thickest veils between man and Allah are the wise man's wisdom, the worshiper's worship, and the devotion of the devout.

Bayazid Bistami

If I only knew that I had taken one single step in sincerity, I would give no value to anything else.

Bayazid Bistami

Not only do beings and things have spirits that in turn take the forms of beings and things, but deeds, words, thoughts, and feelings also have spirits of their own. Thus it may happen that the soul of a beautiful deed may assume the form of an angel.

Sheikh Badruddin

This spirit of divine origin appears in a man as man, in beast as beast, and in plant as plant. And it appears differently even within each species, appearing in each person in a different manner in accordance with his different capacity and predisposition. The spirit neither disappears not diminishes nor changes when the body is destroyed.

The body, until its end, is in continuous transformation, whereas the spirit never changes. It cannot be identified by anything other than the body it inhabits. There is no identification without appearance; therefore, it is essential for the spirit to have a form. Yet if the spirit becomes fully identified with a specific body, it cannot return to its origin.

Sheikh Badruddin

It takes a while longer before the full extent of the miracle that has happened to me today becomes accessible to my conscious knowledge as well. I've often thought about one of the basic requirements of Islam: one must *love* the Prophet (peace be upon him). That always struck me as an impossibility. The way I understand "loving," it's a feeling that develops in the course of contact with another being on the basis of certain shared experiences. How can I feel love for somebody who lived so long ago? With whom I could never have had any contact? A command to show respect and deference toward the Prophet (peace be upon him) would have seemed appropriate to me. But love? My intense involvement with the historical Muhammad had indeed taught the greatest admiration for this extraordinary person, well and good. But the Islamic command to love him, a person long since dead, struck me as impossible, illogical, and unthinkable.

Only now do I see how correct the word *unthinkable* is for this command. Of course love isn't something that could ever be achieved by thinking, by an effort of the will. When it "hits," that is pure grace. Could that be what is meant when my Teacher is always talking about "going through the heart"? Understanding what that means is still impossible for me. But all at once I have been allowed to have the direct, living experience of the "unthinkable."

Ozelsel

There are three agents that destroy religion: an ill-tempered scholar, a tyrannical leader, and an ignorant theologian.

Muhammad

Strength lies not in carrying heavy loads: a crane can do that. Strength's essence is found in taming your temper and anger.

Muhammad

CHAPTER 11

Love

Whatever we wish to know well, we must love. We can't master any field of study—whether music, art, an academic field, or a profession—unless we love what we are studying. Study without love leads to a shallow, superficial understanding. Real mastery comes from love.

For many, Sufism is the path of love. To love others, to love the beauty of this world develops the capacity for love. The more we can love, the more we can love God. To love God is to know God.

Many of us are afraid of love. We have been disappointed before, not only by our romantic loves but also by friends and family we have loved. We can become afraid to open up and love again. There is an old Turkish saying, "The one who was burned by the soup blows on the yogurt." Yet whatever our past hurts and fears of future pain, we must learn to love again. One of the most important functions of a teacher and a Sufi group of sincere seekers is to provide a safe place to risk loving.

We also fear love because it may transform us. And it is so. For the true lover, the sense of self dissolves so that lover, love, and beloved become one. The ego is afraid of losing control, and even more afraid of dissolving, and comes up with reason after reason for refusing to let go, refusing to let ourselves love fully.

We can let ourselves be inspired by the words of those who have become lovers.

⮌

Leave everything and cleave to love! Turn your heart from all else; feel love in your whole being! Take love as your guide to the land of being so that you may reach the True Beloved, enter the Paradise of God's essence, behold the beauty of the Friend, gather the roses of the garden of Union. In the way of love, the lover sacrifices himself but finds the dear one. All the saints who have drunk of the wine of love have sacrificed themselves thus in the way of love.

Sheikh Muzaffer

You may try a hundred things, but love alone will release you from yourself. So never flee from love—not even from love in an earthly guise—for it is a preparation for the supreme Truth. How will you ever read the Koran without first learning the alphabet?

Jami

Love is to see what is good and beautiful in everything. It is to learn from everything, to see the gifts of God and the generosity of God in everything. It is to be thankful for all God's bounties.

This is the first step on the road to the love of God. This is just a seed of love. In time, the seed will grow and become a tree and bear fruit. Then, whoever tastes of that fruit will know what real love is. It will be difficult for those who have tasted to tell of it to those who have not.

Sheikh Muzaffer

Be the captive of Love in order that you may be truly free—free from coldness and the worship of self. Thousands have passed who were wise and learned but who were strangers to Love. No name is left to them, nothing to proclaim their fame and dignity or to relate their history in the march of time. Although you may attempt to do a hundred things in this world, only Love will give you release from the bondage of yourself.

Jami

There is no salvation for the soul
But to fall in Love.
It has to creep and crawl
Among the Lovers first.

Only Lovers can escape
From these two worlds.
This was written in creation.

Only from the Heart
Can you reach the sky.
The rose of Glory
Can only be raised in the Heart.

Rumi

The eyes of the dervish who is a true lover see nothing but God; his heart knows nothing but God. God is the eye by which he sees, the hand with which he holds, and the tongue with which he speaks. Were he not in love, he would pass away. If his heart should be empty of love for as much as a single moment, the dervish could not stay alive. Love is the dervish's life, his health, his comfort. Love ruins the dervish, makes him weep; union with the Beloved makes him flourish, brings him to life.

Sheikh Muzaffer

God's most effective, strongest creation is love.

Bahaeddin, Rumi's father

Those who don't feel this Love
pulling them like a river,
those who don't drink dawn
like a cup of spring water
or take in sunset like supper,
those who don't want to change,

let them sleep.

This Love is beyond the study of theology,
that old trickery and hypocrisy.
If you want to improve your mind that way,

sleep on.

I've given up on my brain.
I've torn the cloth to shreds
and thrown it away.

If you're not completely naked,
wrap your beautiful robe of words
around you,

and sleep.

Rumi

Love makes us speak; love makes us moan; love makes us die;
love brings us to life; love makes us drunk and bewildered; it
sometimes makes one a king. Love and the lover have no rigid
doctrine. Whichever direction the lover takes, he turns toward
his beloved. Wherever he may be, he is with his beloved.
Wherever he goes, he goes with his beloved. He cannot do anything, cannot survive for even one moment, without his
beloved. He constantly recalls his beloved, as his beloved re-

members him. Lover and beloved, rememberer and remembered, are ever in each other's company, always together.

Sheikh Muzaffer

All the atoms of the universe became so many mirrors, each reflecting an aspect of the eternal splendor. A portion fell on the rose, which drove the nightingale mad with love. Its ardor inflamed the candle's cheek, and hundreds of moths came from every side and burned themselves on it. It set the sun ablaze, and made the water lily loom up from the depths.

Jami

By love, bitter things are made sweet and copper turns to gold. By love, the sediment becomes clear and torment is removed. By love, the dead are made to live. By love, the sovereign is made a slave.

This love is the fruit of knowledge. When did folly sit on a throne like this?

The faith of love is separated from all religion. For lovers the faith and the religion is God. O spirit, in striving and seeking become like running water. O reason, at all times be ready to give up mortality for the sake of immortality.

Remember God always, that self may be forgotten, so that your self may be effaced in the One to Whom you pray, without care for who is praying, or the prayer.

Rumi

Love is a special, pleasurable pain. Whoever has this in the heart will know the secret. They will see that everything is Truth, and that everything leads to Truth. There is nothing but Truth. In the realization of that, they will be overcome. They will sink into the sea of Truth.

Sheikh Muzaffer

The whole world is a marketplace for Love,
For naught that is, from Love remains remote.
The Eternal Wisdom made all things in Love.
On Love they all depend, to Love all turn.
The earth, the heavens, the sun, the moon, the stars
The center of their orbit find in Love.
By Love are all bewildered, stupefied,
Intoxicated by the Wine of Love.

From each, Love demands a mystic silence.
What do all seek so earnestly? 'Tis Love.
Love is the subject of their inmost thoughts,
In Love no longer "Thou" and "I" exist,
For self has passed away in the Beloved.
Now will I draw aside the veil from Love,
And in the temple of mine inmost soul
Behold the Friend, Incomparable Love.
He who would know the secret of both worlds
Will find that the secret of them both is Love.

Attar

The secret of madness is the source of reason.
A mature man is insane for Love.
The one who has his Heart together
Is a thousand times stranger to himself.

Rumi

The dervish has no worries and no cares. His sole concern is
God, his pain is God, his remedy is God, his cure is God, his
cause is God. Were he not in love, he would pass away. If his
heart should be devoid of love for as much as a single moment,
the dervish could not stay alive. Love is the dervish's life, his
health, his comfort. Love ruins the dervish, makes him weep;

union makes him flourish, brings him to life. The dervish finds separation in union, union in separation.

Sheikh Muzaffer

Sheikh Uftade had just recovered from an illness. It was winter, and the water was too cold for him to use in his ablution when he got up for his early morning prayer, so his disciple, Hüdai, always got up before his master and warmed some water for him over the fire. One frosty morning Hüdai noticed that his master was already awake. He jumped up with a cry of dismay, hastily grabbed the pitcher of water, and held it tight against his breast. The sheikh rolled up his sleeves and held his arms over the basin, but the water that poured from the pitcher scalded his hand. Staring in amazement at his beloved disciple, he said, "Hüdai, where did you boil this?" Hüdai replied, "On the fire of the heart, my sheikh."

Sheikh Muzaffer

One day, Rabia asked, "Who shall lead us to our Beloved?" and her servant answered, "Our Beloved is with us, but this world cuts us off from Him."

Rabia

Rabia was asked, "Do you love God?"

She answered, "Yes."

"Do you hate the devil?"

She answered, "No, my love of God leaves me no time to hate the devil."

Rabia

Someone asked Rabia, "What is your love for the Prophet like?" She replied, "Truly I love him greatly, but love of the Creator has turned me aside from love of His creatures."

Rabia

A man once fell madly in love with a beautiful woman. He followed her for days and finally went up to her on the street and declared his undying, all-consuming love.

He went on and on, and finally the woman interrupted, "Your words are lovely, but my sister is coming along behind me. She is far more beautiful than I am, and I'm sure that you will prefer her to me."

As the man spun around to look at the beautiful sister, the woman slapped him sharply on the back of his neck. She exclaimed, "I thought you said that your love for me was all-consuming and undying. Some love you have! The instant I mentioned a more beautiful woman, you turned away from me to look at her. You don't even know the meaning of love!"

Sheikh Muzaffer

Bahlul had a reputation for being madly in love with God. We think that we all love God. But Bahlul's kind of love was different indeed. Far different. He conversed with his beloved day and night. It is as if he was in love with the most astonishingly beautiful woman in the universe, and she has stolen his heart and soul totally. He carries her with himself everywhere, talking to her all his waking and even sleeping moments.

One day Bahlul's love for God got so out of hand that he left his home, quit his job, and started wandering—only God knows with what purpose. Since that time, he has become so totally lost in love that he has abandoned all thought of anything but God, ignoring his own appearance and well-being. The man has no time for himself, and that's why his clothes are so ragged and his hair and beard have grown so long. "Any moment that is not spent paying attention to the Beloved," Bahlul has said, "is a moment wasted."

Attar

A person often remembers the object of his love. One who is a lover of God also remembers Him, always and everywhere. On the bough of the beloved's rosebush, love's nightingale sings its love incessantly.

Sheikh Muzaffer

The heart that is free of love sickness isn't a heart at all. The body deprived of the pangs of love is nothing but clay and water.

Jami

Sight is not the only way that love enters the heart; it often happens that love is born of the spoken word. The echo of beauty entering the ear may rob heart and soul of peace and reason.

Jami

If love manifests itself within you, it has its origins in beauty. You are nothing but a mirror in which beauty is reflected. Because beauty and its reflection are both from that one source, it is both treasure and treasure-house.

Jami

Whatever you taste of love, in whatever manner, in whatever degree—it is a tiny part of Divine Love. Love between men and women is also a part of that Divine Love. But sometimes the beloved becomes a curtain between love and realization of true love. One day that curtain will lift and then the real Beloved, the real goal will appear in all Divine glory.

What is important is to have this feeling of love in your heart, in whatever form and shape. It is also important that you be loved. It is easier to love than to be the beloved. If you have been in love you will certainly reach the Beloved one day.

Sheikh Muzaffer

When a heart finds repose with the beloved, how should it ever desire another? Did you ever see a moth flying to the sun, when all its hope lies in the candle flame? It is pointless to spread a hundred bunches of fragrant herbs before the nightingale, who only wishes for the rose's balmy breath. Once the water lily has been caressed by the sweet warmth of the sun, will it ever show any interest in the moon? When a soul thirsts for a draught of clear water, it has no use for sugar.

Jami

O Lord, nourish me not with love but with the desire for love.
Ibn 'Arabi

How lucky the heart where love makes its home, for love makes it forget the cares of the world! Love is like a bolt of lightning, which sets fire to patience and reason and reduces them to nothing.

The lover becomes careless of his own safety. Mountains of blame weigh no more for him than a straw; criticism only increases his passion.

Jami

Love makes us penetrate the mountains. Love makes us reach the goal. Love causes ecstasy. Ecstasy, the state in which love and longing overwhelm the soul, gives the taste to the *dhikr* [remembrance] of the worshiper. Such a state is this that, if at that moment one of the worshiper's limbs were to be cut off or broken, he would not even feel that pain amid the joy and delight occasioned by his vision of the everlasting Beauty.

Sheikh Muzaffer

Love solves all problems, opens all closed doors.
Sheikh Muzaffer

All that the Beloved does is beloved.

Kashani

The place of Love is the heart, and the heart is pure gold. The divine majesty polished it by gazing upon it, making it bright and pure. The traces of the lights of the beauty of unqualified Love appear in the mirrors of pious hearts. Human love subsists through God's Love.

Samani

Let the eye of your heart be opened that you may see the spirit and behold invisible things.

If you set your face toward the region where Love reigns, you will see the whole universe laid out as a rose garden. What you see, your heart will wish to have, and what your heart seeks to possess, that you will see. If you penetrate to the middle of each mote in the sunbeams, you will find a sun within.

Give all that you possess to Love. If your spirit is dissolved in the flames of Love, you will see that Love is the alchemy for spirit.

You will journey beyond the narrow limitations of time and place and will pass into the infinite spaces of the Divine World. What ear has not heard, that you will hear, and what no eye has seen, you shall behold. Finally, you shall be brought to that high Abode, where you will see One only, beyond the world and all worldly creatures. To that One you shall devote the love of both heart and soul until, with the eye that knows no doubt, you will see plainly that "One is and there is nothing save God alone."

Ahmad Hatif

Caliph Harun al-Rashid's favorite concubine was very plain, but he preferred her to all of her beautiful rivals. When asked for a reason, the Caliph offered a demonstration.

He summoned all his concubines and then opened the door of his private treasure chamber, which was filled with gold and jewels. He told the women that they could take whatever they desired. They all ran to gather up as much as they could, except his favorite, who did not even enter the treasure chamber.

"Why don't you take something for yourself?" asked the Caliph.

The woman replied, "All I want is to serve you. You are all I need. You are the one I love, and your love is all the reward I want."

Sheikh Muzaffer

Since I have heard of the world of Love,
I've spent my life, my heart
And my eyes this way.
I used to think that love
And beloved are different.
I know they are the same.

Rumi

Listen friends, love is like the sun.
The heart without love is nothing but a piece of stone.

Kabakli

PART 4

Sufi Teachers

CHAPTER 12

Teachers and Students

A synonym for Sufism in Arabic is "path" (or tariqah). This term does not mean a road that anyone can follow. It refers to a path in the desert from one oasis to the next. It is a trackless path; the sands shift constantly. You need a guide to get to that next oasis because, unless you have traveled that way often, you could never find your way by yourself. A Sufi teacher is a guide who has traveled the spiritual path, who knows the way and its pitfalls and dangers.

There is a famous story of Nasruddin, a humorous teaching figure popular throughout the Middle East, that illustrates the position of the guide. A group of young people came to Nasruddin's house and asked him to be their teacher. He agreed and told them to accompany him to the Sufi lodge for their first lesson. Nasruddin then proceeded to get on his donkey, riding backward, and led the group across town. The townspeople all laughed at Nasruddin and jeered at the group as gullible fools for following him.

By the time they got to the Sufi lodge, most of the group was gone. One of those who remained asked, "Nasruddin, why were you riding backward?" Nasruddin answered, "Well, you know it isn't polite for students to walk in front of their teacher. And it wouldn't *have been right for me to turn my back on all of you. So this was the only way to do it!"*

This story has many levels of meaning. Nasruddin demonstrates his own disregard of conventional opinion while he tests his students' sincerity and perseverance. He also models the role of a real teacher, who knows the path and whose main attention is on his students. In addition, he illustrates the need for mutual respect between teacher and student.

This chapter is filled with examples of the many nuances of teacher-student relationships. Some may seem puzzling or even objectionable. Others may be inspiring. Each example offers different lessons.

⇔

The true teacher knocks down the idol that the student makes of him.

Rumi

On all paths of spiritual training, the teacher is of central importance. He or she embodies the teaching as a living representation of the tradition. He or she helps the student to grow beyond the boundaries of self. Because each person can only, by definition, operate *inside* his or her current limits, outside intervention is indispensable to make the "breakthrough." My Teacher depicted this state of things with the following analogy: "You can give yourself first aid, putting a bandage on a wound. But you can't operate on yourself."

The fundamental changes that the path requires in the student's worldview and behavior resemble a major operation. The very personality features that the student holds tightest to, with which he or she most strongly identifies on this level, are also the ones that prevent the student from fully becoming what he or she potentially is. [Rumi has written:] "It is necessary to make so great an effort that you are not left standing, in order that you may recognize what it is that will remain."

Ozelsel

The sheikh was a man of pleasing countenance and graceful appearance. He was long in thinking and deliberating and short in words. He never inclined toward anything of the world or any of its vanities, never attempted to amass wealth. Whatever was given in charity to him, he immediately distributed among the dervishes, never accepting more than a single portion for himself.

Masum 'Ali Shah

A fall of seven floors is a gentle drop compared with falling from the heart and affection of the spiritual guide.

Sheikh Muzaffer

When I stood in front of him—or any other of my teachers—I would start trembling like a leaf in the wind; my voice would change and my limbs would start knocking together. When he noticed this, he would show kindness toward me and make a special effort to help me relax, but that only served to increase the awe and veneration he inspired in me.

Shibli

One day I went to see my teacher Abu l-Abbas while I was in this state [of confusion].

I was troubled at the sight of men disobeying God. He said to me, "My companion, occupy yourself with God!" I left him and went to Sheikh Abu Imran, still in the same state of mind. He said, "Occupy yourself with your soul!" I replied, "Master, I am in a state of perplexity. Sheikh Abu l-Abbas tells me to occupy myself with God, but you tell me to occupy myself with my soul. And yet both of you are guides toward God!" Abu Imran started weeping and said to me, "My friend, Abu l-Abbas has directed you toward God, and the return is to Him. Each of us has directed you in accordance with his spiritual state. I hope that God will make me reach to the station of Abu l-Abbas. So listen to him. That will be better for you and for me."

I returned to Sheikh Abu l-Abbas and told him what Abu Imran had said. He said to me, "Take account of his advice, for he has pointed out to you the path, whereas I have pointed out to you the Companion. You should therefore act in accordance with what he has told you and in accordance with what I have told you.

Ibn 'Arabi

The following two stories tell different versions of the first meeting of Rumi with his spiritual guide, Shems, who helped Rumi transform from a dry theology professor into one of the world's greatest mystical poets:

One day Rumi was sitting in his personal library with a group of his students gathered around him for his lecture. Suddenly, Shems entered uninvited. He pointed to the books that were stacked in a corner and asked Rumi, "What are these?"

Rumi, who judged Shems from his appearance to be a beggar, answered, "You would not understand." He had not even finished his sentence when flames of fire started to rise from the books in the corner. Frightened, Rumi cried out, "What is this?"

Shems replied calmly, "Nor would you understand this." So saying, he left the room.

Rumi

One day Rumi was riding on horseback with a crowd of his students following him. He stopped at the university where he was to give his regular class. A wretched-looking figure followed Rumi into the classroom. It was Shems, who asked Rumi, "Who was greater—Bayazid Bistami or the prophet Muhammad?"

Rumi, who felt the energy of Shems' glance piercing his soul, replied, "The prophet Muhammad was greater."

Shems said, "Did not the Prophet say, 'We have not known You as You deserve to be known,' whereas Bayazid exclaimed,

'How great is my station; glory be upon me who is exalted, whose dignity is upraised'?" Shems saw that Rumi was unable to answer and explained that Bayazid's thirst for God was quenched after drinking a mouthful, but the Prophet's thirst was never quenched, for he was always thirsty for more water of divine knowledge.

Finding himself overwhelmed by Shems' powerful words, Rumi fell to the ground at Shems' feet, crying until he lost consciousness. When Rumi came to, his head was on Shems' lap. Shortly afterward, the two men went into seclusion together for three months.

Rumi

Bahlul, the wise fool, used to disguise his wisdom behind a veil of craziness. He came and went freely in the palace of Harun al-Rashid, who valued his guidance.

One day, Bahlul found the caliph's throne unoccupied, so he promptly sat down on it. To sit on the sultan's throne was considered a major crime and might even be punished by death. The palace guard grabbed Bahlul, dragged him off the throne, and beat him severely. His cries of pain brought the caliph running to the scene.

Bahlul was still sobbing loudly as Harun asked his soldiers the reason for the uproar. As he turned to console Bahlul, the caliph said to the soldiers, "For shame! The poor wretch is crazy. Would any sane man sit on the royal throne?" He said to Bahlul, "Don't cry! Don't worry. Wipe the tears from your eyes." Bahlul said, "O Caliph, it is not their blows that make me weep; it is for your sake I am crying." "For my sake?" exclaimed Harun. "Why should you weep over me?" Bahlul replied, "O Caliph! I sat on your throne once, and what a beating I got for sitting there for just a few moments. But you, you have occupied this throne for twenty years. What kind of a beating will you be in for, I wonder? It is that thought that has me weeping."

Harun al-Rashid was dismayed. Now it was his turn to weep. "What can I do?" he asked. Bahlul ran off through the palace, crying, "Justice, justice!"

Sheikh Muzaffer

Shems asked a sheikh, "What are you doing?"

"I am looking at the moon's reflection in this lake," replied the sheikh.

"Why don't you look directly at the sky? Are you so blind that you do not see the true object in all you contemplate?"

Shems' reply had such an effect on the sheikh that he asked Shems to accept him as his disciple.

"You do not have the strength to bear my company," replied Shems.

"The strength is within me," said the sheikh. "Please accept me."

"Then bring me a pitcher of wine, and we will drink together in the Baghdad market."

Fearing public opinion (because alcohol is forbidden by Islam), the sheikh replied, "I cannot do this."

Shems shouted, "You are too timid for me. You haven't the strength to be among the intimate friends of God. I seek only those who know how to reach the Truth."

Shems Tabrizi

How can you criticize your brother's faults if your words create a rift between the two of you? You must realize that alienation of the heart only results from mentioning a fault already known to your brother. To draw his attention to what he is unaware of is compassion itself.

Someone who draws your attention to a unpleasant habit, or a negative feature of your character, so that you can cleanse yourself of it is like one who warns you of a snake or scorpion

under your robe—he has shown concern lest you perish. If you
disapprove of that, how great is your folly!

al-Ghazzali

The first Sufi lodge was built at Ramla in Syria. One day a
Christian prince had gone out hunting. While on the road he
saw two Sufis meet and embrace each other. They then sat down
in that same spot and, spreading out what food they had, ate together. Their affection for each other pleased him, and he called
out to one of them and asked him who the other was. The man
replied, "I don't know."

The prince said, "What relation is he to you?"

The man answered, "None at all."

The prince asked, "From what place has he come?"

He said, "I don't know that either."

The prince said, "Why then do you show each other such affection?"

The dervish replied, "He belongs to my Way."

The prince asked, "Have you any place where you can meet
together?" When the dervish said they had not, the prince said,
"I will build you such a place," and so he did.

Margaret Smith

On the Day of Judgment each soul will be asked what deeds it
brought with it, what good deeds it has accomplished, to gain
admittance to Paradise. On the divine balance scale, all our good
deeds will be weighed against our sins and errors.

When your deeds are weighed and you are found lacking, as
so many of us will be, you will turn to your husband or wife and
ask if he or she can spare any good deeds to help you in your
plight. Absorbed in their own judgment, they will say, "What
about me? Who will help *me?*" You will turn to your father and
mother, and they too will say, "I need help. Will anyone help *me?*"

Then your sheikh or one of your brother or sister dervishes will appear and say to you, "Take *all* my good deeds. It is enough for me if *you* enter Paradise."

Sheikh Muzaffer

An ailing king summoned a physician-sage to treat his illness. The sage refused to come. The king had his soldiers seize the physician and bring him to the palace.

The king said, "I have brought you here because I am suffering from a strange paralysis. If you cure me, I will reward you. If not, I will kill you."

The physician said, "In order to treat you, I need complete privacy." So the king sent everyone out of the room. Then the physician took out a knife and said, "Now I shall take my revenge for your threatening me." He advanced on the king. Terrified, the king jumped up and ran around the room, forgetting his paralysis in his need to escape the seemingly crazed physician.

The sage fled the palace one step ahead of the guards. The king never realized that he had been cured by the only method that could have been effective.

Traditional

Shibli entered a profound mystical state and was placed in an asylum as a madman. As soon as they heard, his shocked disciples come to visit him.

Shibli asked, "Who are you?"

"We are some of those who love and follow you."

Shibli began throwing stones at his students. They began to run away, crying, "It's true. Shibli really has gone crazy."

Then Shibli called out to them, "Didn't I hear you say that you loved me? You could not even bear a stone or two before running away. What became of that sincere love you claimed you had for me? Did your love fly away with a couple of stones?

If you had really loved me, you would have patiently endured the little bit of discomfort I caused you."

Shibli

I was companion to Abdullah al-Razi as he was going into the desert. He said, "Either you or I must act as leader." So I said, "I would rather that you be the leader."

"Then you must obey me," he said.

"Very well," I agreed.

Then he took a bag, filled it with provisions, and carried it on his back. When I said, "Hand it over to me." He replied, "Did you not say, 'You are the leader'? Well then, you must obey me."

That night we were caught by the rain. He stood at my head until morning, shielding me from the rain with a cloak he wore, while I sat there, saying to myself, "If only I had died sooner than said, 'You be leader!'"

Abu Ali al-Ribati

The eight duties of a teacher are

1. To be sympathetic to students and treat them as his or her own children. The teacher must care about the students' welfare as mothers and fathers care for their own children.

2. To refuse any remuneration for his or her services and accept neither reward nor thanks.

3. Not to withhold any advice from the student or allow the student to work at any level unless qualified for it.

4. To use sympathetic and indirect suggestions in dissuading students from bad habits, rather than open, harsh criticism. Open criticism incites defiance and stubbornness.

5. When teaching a given discipline, not to belittle the value of other disciplines or teachers.

6. To limit the students to what they can understand and not require of them anything that is beyond their intellectual capacity.

7. To give backward students only such things as are clear and suitable to their limited understanding. Everyone believes him- or herself capable of mastering every discipline, no matter how complex, and the most simple and foolish are usually most pleased with their intellect.

8. To do what one teaches and not allow one's actions to contradict one's words.

al-Ghazzali

Maturity cannot be achieved alone. There is a need for guidance and discipline. The path is unknown, the night is dark, and the road is full of danger. Dangers include preoccupation with self-ishness, false visions, misinterpretations of mystical states, arrest in development, fixation in a particular state, appeal to various drugs to create false mystical experiences, and, not infrequently, overwhelming anxiety and insanity.

Mohammed Shafii

A young man became the student of a sheikh and was given the job of cleaning the latrines. His mother, a wealthy physician, asked the sheikh to give her tender young son some other job and sent the sheikh twelve Ethiopian slaves to clean the outhouses. The sheikh replied, "You are a physician. If your son had an inflammation of the gall bladder, should I give the medicine to a Ethiopian slave instead of giving it to him?"

Jami

Real friendship among brothers and sisters on the Sufi path includes the following eight responsibilities:

1. *Material aid.* Help your companions with food, or money, or other things they need for their own survival or development.

2. *Personal support.* If they are sick, visit them; if they are busy, help them; if they have forgotten, remind them.

3. *Respect.* Do not complain of their faults to them or to others. Do not give advice when you know it cannot be acted upon.
4. *Praise and attention.* Praise the good qualities of your companions, and let them know that you care for them.
5. *Forgiveness.* Forgive your companions for their failings.
6. *Prayer.* Pray for the well-being of your companions with the same fervor you pray for your own well-being.
7. *Loyalty.* Be firm in your friendships so that you can be depended on by those who put their trust in you.
8. *Relief from discomfort.* Do not create awkward or difficult situations that involve your companions. Do not be a burden to others.

al-Ghazzali

Then there arises the question of how to find the real teacher. Very often people are in doubt; they do not know whether the teacher they see is a true or a false teacher. Frequently a person comes into contact with a false teacher in this world where there is so much falsehood. But at the same time a real seeker, one who is not false to himself, will always meet with the truth, with the real, because it is his own real faith, his own sincerity in earnest seeking that will become his torch.

The real teacher is within, the lover of reality is one's own sincere self, and if one is really seeking truth, sooner or later one will certainly find a true teacher. And supposing one came into contact with a false teacher, what then? Then the real One will turn the false teacher also into a real teacher, because Reality is greater than falsehood.

Hazrat Inayat Khan

Many teachers talk about teachings. The best teachers study their pupils as well. Most important, teachers should be studied.

Musa Kasin

It is easy to be a sheikh and difficult to be a dervish. The founders of two of the great Sufi orders, Abdul Qadir al-Jilani and Ahmed al-Rifai, were sitting together when someone ran in and told Abdul Qadir al-Jilani that one of the teachers he had sent to India had died, and that the dervishes there asked him to send a new sheikh. Abdul Qadir al-Jilani turned to Ahmed al-Rifai and said, "I'm glad they asked for a sheikh, because if they had asked for a dervish, either you or I would have had to go."

Sheikh Muzaffer

One reason for the institution of a Guide is that he knows when to direct the disciple's effort and work and when not to direct it. He also knows the kind of effort and work that each individual should do. Only the ignorant mistake any work for useful work.

Palawan-i-Zaif

The lovers' success is most enhanced by affection for their spiritual guide, by loving performance of their service to him or her, and by prayers and service for the guide. Affection for the guide, arising from deep within the pupil, is like the spiritual river flowing in the inner being of the guide. Indeed, this abundant flow causes the bounty of the spiritual guide to spill over to the pupil. Thus the current of this bounty ebbs or flows according to the pupil's affection for the guide.

In short, the pupil should love the guide with a genuine, sincere, and unhypocritical affection. It should be well understood that there is a path from heart to heart. Therefore, pupils are repaid for their love and affection toward their guide by the blessings they experience from the guide. This has stood the test of centuries and constitutes the essence of practical truths.

Sheikh Muzaffer

A young man came to Junaid and wished to become his student. He said, "You have been recommended as an expert on pearls [of wisdom]. Please give me one, or sell it to me."

Junaid replied, "You could not afford the price if I sold it, and if I gave you one for nothing, you will not realize its value. You must do as I have done. Dive into the Sea and wait patiently until you obtain your pearl."

Attar

In the absence of the sheikh, the pupils should conduct themselves exactly as they would in the sheikh's presence, should perform their duties fully, and should be extremely polite and well behaved everywhere and in all that they do. The belief and conviction that, although we cannot see Almighty God, God sees us however we are and whatever we are doing transforms our submission into active goodness and brings us to the condition of perfect belief.

Sheikh Muzaffer

Eight Duties of Brotherhood

1. At the lowest level, give spontaneously from your surplus; at the middle level, treat your brother as an equal partner; at the highest level, prefer him to yourself.

2. Spontaneously provide for your brother's personal needs, giving them priority over your own. At the lowest level, attend plentifully when asked, with joy and cheerfulness, showing pleasure and gratitude; at the middle level, treat the person as an equal partner; at the higher level, prefer the other to yourself.

3. For your brother's sake, feign ignorance of his faults, even if you must lie to do so.

4. Express affection to your brother; ask agreeably about his circumstances; praise him, and convey the praises of others; defend him in his absence; instruct him as needed in worldly and spiritual matters. Take him to task if he does not act appropriately, but only in private. Avoid alienation by not pointing out faults that are known to your brother; instead,

exercise compassion and point out only faults not known to him.

5. If someone errs in his duty as a brother, forgiveness and patience are always the proper course.

6. Pray for your brother, that he may have all he wishes for himself, his family, and his dependents, both during his life and after his death.

7. Show "steadfastness in love." Such love requires you to care for a brother's children after his death. Loyalty includes preventing a relationship from degenerating into one of humility; not agreeing to something contrary to religious principles; not listening to gossip about him; and not befriending his enemy.

8. Relieve your brother from discomfort and inconvenience. For example, do not ask him for services or require that he be polite.

al-Ghazzali

Love all and hate none.
Mere talk of peace will avail you naught.
Mere talk of God and religion will not take you far.
Be a blazing fire of truth,
be a beauteous blossom of love
and be a soothing balm of peace.
With your spiritual light, dispel the darkness of ignorance;
dissolve the clouds of discord and war
and spread goodwill, peace, and harmony among the people.
Never seek any help, charity, or favors
from anybody except God.
Never go to the courts of kings,
but never refuse to bless and help the needy and the poor,
the widow, and the orphan, if they come to your door.
This is your mission, to serve the people . . .
Carry it out dutifully and courageously,

so that I, as your spiritual teacher,
may not be ashamed of any shortcomings on your part
before the Almighty God and our holy predecessors
in the Sufi Order
on the Day of Judgment.

Hazrat Khuaja

The hardest hazard facing disciples of "great" teachers: that each
and all tend to worship the teacher and not live according the
principles he or she announces.

Jami

I feel like a gardener who planted a bunch of seeds and nothing
came up; and again the next year he planted a bunch more seeds
and nothing came up; and again the next year more seeds and
with the same results; and so on and on and on. And then this
year, he planted a bunch of seeds: not only did they all come up,
but all the seeds from the previous year came up and all the
seeds from the year before, and so on. So, I've just been franti-
cally running around trying to harvest all the plants until Allah
came to me and said, "Don't worry. Harvest what you can and
leave the rest to Me."

Sam Lewis

Saints, I see the world is mad.
If I tell the truth they rush to beat me,
if I lie they trust me.
I've seen the pious Hindus, rule followers,
early morning bath takers—
killing souls, they worship rocks.
They know nothing.
I've seen plenty of Muslim teachers, holy men
reading their holy books
and teaching their pupils techniques.
They know just as much.

And posturing yogis, hypocrites,
hearts crammed with pride,
praying to brass, to stones, reeling
with pride in their pilgrimage,
fixing their caps and prayer beads,
painting their brow-marks and arm-marks,
braying their hymns and their couplets,
reeling. They never heard of soul.
The Hindu says Ram is the Beloved,
The Turk says Rahim.
Then they kill each other.
No one knows the secret.
They buzz their mantras from house to house,
puffed with pride.
The pupils drown along with their gurus.
In the end they're very sorry.
Kabir says, listen saints:
they're all deluded!
Whatever I say, nobody gets it.
It's so simple.

Kabir

As marble on a dome
rolls down,
on a fool's heart, the word
won't pause.
Man in his stupid acts:
iron mail from head to toe.
Why bother to raise your bow?
No arrow can pierce that.

Kabir

Junaid had decided not to speak on Sufism as long as his master,
Sari, was alive. One night he dreamed that the Prophet said to

him, "O Junaid, speak to people, for it is God's wish that you show people the Path by speaking to them."

Junaid thereupon woke up, feeling very proud and believing that he was spiritually superior to his master. However, in the morning he got a message from Sari that said, "You didn't listen to your disciples' request, nor did you to mine. But now that the Prophet has asked you to give talks, obey him."

Upon hearing this, Junaid said, he knew that his master was indeed far more developed than he was. He went to Sari and asked, "How did you know that the Prophet has asked me to speak?"

Sari answered, "I dreamed that God said to me that he had sent the Prophet to you to ask you."

Hujwiri

A thief entered the house of a Sufi and found nothing there to steal. As he was leaving, the dervish, sensing his disappointment, threw him the blanket on which he had been lying.

Sa'di

The two horseman rode forth in the early morning hours. One of these riders was blind. Having dropped his whip, he dismounted and began groping around for it. There was a chill in the air, and a snake had coiled up and gone to sleep at that spot. The creature was rigid from the cold, so that it felt like a whip when the blind man touched it with his hand. He picked it up, remounted, and caught up with his comrade, who asked where he had been. The blind rider explained that he had dropped his old whip, but had found a better one lying on the ground. His friend warned him that his new "whip" was really a snake, but the blind man stubbornly refused to throw it away. Eventually the sun came up. The sun's warmth roused the creature, which inflicted a fatal bite on the blind horseman.

Sheikh Muzaffer

Bayazid Bistami, sitting at the feet of his teacher, suddenly was asked, "Bayazid, fetch me that book sitting by the window."

"The window? Which window? asked Bayazid.

"Why," said the master, "you have been coming all this time and did not see the window?"

"No," replied Bayazid. "What have I to do with the window? When I am before you, I close my eyes to everything else. I have not come to stare about."

"Because that is so," said the teacher, "go back to your own city. Your work is completed."

Bayazid Bistami

We are the means of reaching the goal. It is necessary that seekers should cut themselves away from us and think only of the goal.

Bahauddin Naqshband

O you who seek truth and the real reality, come, have pity on yourself. Find a cure for the sickness of ignorance by which you take your imagination to be reality and from which you suffer all your life. Search for a cure day and night, until you feel secure from all that you fear.

You do see some people at peace, saved from the disease of ambition though they have less than you do—while you are in pain and oppressed by all that you have.

A day will certainly come when you will regret all this, but it may be too late. Start to learn, and leave this ignorance that you take for knowledge. After you find the perfect teacher for you, let your love for him be your guide. It is from him that you will learn to find yourself and find the truth in your own being.

Sheikh Muzaffer

People think that a sheikh should show miracles and manifest illumination. The requirement of a teacher, however, is only that he should possess all that the disciple needs.

Ibn 'Arabi

There was a ruler who had a servant for whom he cared more than his other servants; none of them was more valuable or more handsome than this one, so he wanted to make clear to them the superiority of this servant over the others. One day he was riding with his entourage. In the distance was a snow-capped mountain. The ruler looked at that snow and bowed his head. The servant galloped off on his horse. The people did not know why he galloped off. In a short time he came back with some snow, and the ruler asked him, "How did you know I wanted snow?"

The servant replied, "Because you looked at it, and the look of the sultan comes only with firm intention."

So the ruler said, "I accord him special favor and honor, because for every person there is an occupation, and his occupation is observing my glances and watching my states of being attentively."

Qushayri

Whoever travels without a guide
needs two hundred years for a two-day journey.

Rumi

On the long hard road that faces the disciple he needs a guide, the sheikh, for it is dangerous to wander alone. The prophets and saints are the soul doctors who can successfully diagnose the sicknesses and weaknesses of the soul, and if a person entrusts himself to them with no questions, they can heal these as well. However, their healing methods are sometimes quite severe. They show the wanderers that they must "die before their death," that they must completely lose their own being.

Annemarie Schimmel

Junaid once saw a man strolling by the edge of the River Euphrates. He asked him why he was strolling there. "I am waiting for a boat to ferry me across to the other shore," the man replied.

"Come," said Junaid, "let me take you across." When the fellow asked him how he could do that, he said, "By remembering Allah." Then he asked, "Take care not to say anything except 'As the Sheikh says.'"

He took the man by the hand, and they started walking on the water together. The venerable Junaid was saying, "Allah, Allah," while the fellow beside him kept repeating the words "As the Sheikh says, as the Sheikh says."

They were halfway across, and the venerable Junaid still went on saying, "O Allah, O Allah, O All-Powerful, O All-Powerful!" The other man began to wonder why he should confine himself to saying, "As the Sheikh says." He decided to try invoking Allah, too, but as soon as he said, "O Allah, O All-Powerful," he began sinking into the river.

The venerable Junaid pulled him to safety, then chided him: "Do you think yourself competent to mention the names of Allah? Because I knew your mouth was not ready for that, I told you to say nothing but 'As the Sheikh says.'"

Sheikh Muzaffer

One day, Sultan Mahmud of Ghazna handed a priceless cup to one of his ministers, saying, "Break it!" "But, sire," protested the minister, "this is a china cup of great value. How could I break it?" "Very well, that's fine," said the Sultan Mahmud, handing the cup to another minister and another and another. All objected to breaking the cup. The Sultan then passed it to Ayaz, his close companion, telling him to break it. Ayaz did not hesitate one moment before dashing the cup to the ground, where it shattered. "Wasn't it a precious cup?" the Sultan asked him. "Yes," replied Ayaz. "It was very valuable indeed. But your word is worth more to me than this cup. I would sooner break a hundred precious cups like this rather than give offense to you."

Sheikh Muzaffer

O ignorant fool. You fail to take these words to heart and prefer to be in your private cell in the company of your mind and desire and passions. First of all, you need to seek the company of true sheikhs. You need to conquer your mind, desires, karmic habits, and everything else besides God Almighty. You need to become a regular attendant at their doorsteps—I mean the true sheikhs. Learn at their hands. Only after that may you move to your hermitage and be alone with God Almighty. Once you satisfy these conditions, then you may become a cure for people's illnesses, a guide by God's leave. However, your tongue sounds pious, but your heart is rebellious. Your tongue sings God's praises, but your heart protests against His decree. Outwardly you are a Muslim, but inwardly you are a disbeliever. Outwardly you are a monotheist, but inwardly you are a polytheist. Outwardly you are an ascetic and religious, but inwardly you are like mildew on bathroom walls, a lock at the door of a garbage dump.

Abdul Qadir al-Jilani

PART 5

Sufism in Action

CHAPTER 13

Practices

Imagine how it would feel to enter the weight room of a modern exercise club with no understanding of what you see before you. More than a dozen mechanical devices stand in rows, mutely offering to help you become stronger, trimmer, and more vital. Which ones do you use? In what order? How much weight do you load on each? How many repetitions should you do? On another floor there is a swimming pool; outside there is a running track. As if that's not enough to confuse you, you look in the next room. There are treadmills, moving stairways, and stationary bicycles. A room farther on is wall to wall with mats. Pinned on the wall are class schedules for tai chi, stretching, two forms of yoga, and three levels of aerobics. As time passes and you become familiar with the routines on the machines and begin to make progress, new questions arise: What changes should you make in the order of weights to use? How many more repetitions? And so on.

Without guidance, without the ability to discriminate, without some form of help, you can easily waste your time or even hurt yourself.

In any living spiritual tradition, there exist as many practices as there are physical exercises and kinds of equipment in a health club. Those who have achieved some level of enlightenment will almost always feel a need to pass on to others those practices that proved to be most beneficial for their own growth. Students will also ask for help from those who have gone before. From this combination of needs and generosity, whole systems of teaching and learning evolve.

Muhammad lays out the five pillars of Islam; Jesus suggests the Lord's Prayer. Centuries later, the Russian Orthodox Church develops the so-called Jesus Prayer. The Hindu tradition develops myriad forms of yoga, and Buddhists teach a wide range of meditative methods. Every practice is a result of a living teacher, a given need, and a solution correct for some people in that culture at that time.

The practices included here are drawn from a variety of Sufi teachings and may be used as introductions to ways of knowing, as gifts to yourself.

Consider each of these practices. Listen to your heart. If it says, "This is for you now," follow that. Let one practice lead you to another, and to another. Eventually you may be drawn more deeply to a specific teaching tradition and to the blessing of a living teacher.

⤳

Someone asked what there was that was superior to prayer. One answer is that "the soul" of prayer is better than prayer. The second answer is that faith is better than prayer.

Prayer consists of five-times-a-day performance, whereas faith is continuous. Prayer can be dropped for a valid excuse and may be postponed by license; faith cannot be dropped for any excuse and may not be postponed by license. Again, faith without prayer is beneficial, whereas prayer without faith confers no benefit.

Rumi

The practice of breathing in and out of the phrase "Toward the One" can be done at almost any time. One should breathe in a most natural fashion, without attempting to alter the breath in any way. You simply become one with your breath in whatever condition it may be in. The thought and feeling of oneness held in such a fashion allows a person to become united with whatever space or situation he finds himself in. Gradually the boundaries of one's being dissolve. External distractions are overcome by merging with them, including them in overall compass by your being.

Pir Villayat Khan

After the prophet Muhammad and his followers had been successful in securing the Arabian peninsula from external enemies so that they could practice their religion, he said, "We have been successful in the lesser holy war against external enemies; now it is time to take up the greater holy war against those enemies within our own selves, against hatred and jealousy and greed, and so on." It is with this kind of consciousness that this meditation is undertaken.

One begins by simply watching the breath, gradually refining it and making it rhythmical throughout. Consciousness is focused on the heart center in the middle of the breast. You feel your breath gradually massaging and soothing this center of feeling. After doing this for a few minutes until it is a natural process with no mental strain, one moves to the next phase of meditation. One then internally looks into one's heart and feels the impressions that are lodged therein. There may be the surface impressions of the day, the mundane worries of one's existence. One notices and releases each and all of these; they are released by the gentle massaging action of the breath on the heart. As surface impressions are released, deeper impressions make themselves known. One may come face-to-face with a grudge against someone, with an impression of rejection and self-pity, with deeply ingrained emotions of fear or anger. Whatever impression comes up, you face it forthrightly, shining the light of your consciousness on it, continuing the massaging action of the breath (which may have the name of ALLAH inhaled and exhaled on it). You may come upon impressions that resist your efforts; they have lain for so long in your heart that a rusting process has set in. Be assured that by patient effort and trust in Allah, even the most persistent impression can be released, if not in one meditation, then in one hundred and one perhaps. This process has been called Polishing the Lamp of the Heart.

An essential thing about this practice is that all external judgment is suspended. Instead of trying to correct the person or situation on the outside, one gently and patiently massages and releases this impression inside oneself.

Wali Ali

I performed the ablutions, as Hamid has taught me. He had said, "If you do not have water, then wash with sand; and if you do not have sand, then wash with a stone; if a stone is not available, then cleanse yourself with intention so that you approach the moment as free of the past as possible."

Reshad Feild

We must always be in a state of preparation. Preparation is the art of staying awake. If you are awake, then one day you may see into the real world. You cannot expect to come into that world if you walk around like a sleepwalker in a dream. You cannot wake up by reading books that tell you you are asleep. You may not even wake up just because a teacher tells you that you are asleep. You can only wake up if you want to, and so begin to work on yourself to cut away all the rubbish in order to come upon the nature of who and what you are.

Reshad Feild

He then taught me an exercise for what he called "reversing spacing," which involved sitting very still, with all attention focused in the center of the chest, and slowly surrendering and realizing that instead of looking you are being observed, instead of hearing you are being heard, instead of touching you are being touched, instead of tasting you are food for and are being tasted. "So make yourself good tasting," he said. "Finally, allow yourself to be breathed. Abandon yourself completely in trust, and in the realization that you are powerless in the face of God, the First Cause."

Reshad Feild

Be wary, my friend. The angel of death can come while you are only chalking out programs of meditation. Whatever you can do to make initiation and spiritual progress, do it today.

Traditional

Let your heart be in such a state that the existence or nonexistence of anything is the same. Then sit alone in a quiet place, free of any preoccupation, even the reciting of the Koran or thinking about its meaning. Let nothing besides God enter you mind. Once you are seated in this manner, say, "*Allah, Allah,*" keeping your thought on these words.

al-Ghazzali

When I was three years old, I used to say the midnight prayer, having watched my maternal uncle doing this. One day he said to me, "Do you not remember God, your Creator?" and I asked, "How should I remember Him?"

"When you put on your bedclothes, say in your heart three times, without moving your tongue, 'God is with me. God beholds me. God watches over me.'"

This I did for several nights, telling him what I had done. Then he instructed me to say the same words seven times each night, which I did, and then eleven times, upon which I felt a sweetness growing in my heart.

When a year had passed, my uncle said to me, "Keep doing what I have told you until you enter your grave, for it will help you in this world and the next." I continued to do it several years, finding a sweetness within myself, until my uncle said, "Sahl! If God is with somebody and beholds him and watches over him, can he then disobey him? You should never do so."

al-Tustari

The disciple's attempt to purify the heart is like the person ordered to uproot a tree. However much he reflects and struggles to do so, he is unable. So he says to himself, "I'll wait until I'm more powerful and then uproot it." But the longer he waits and leaves the tree to grow, the larger and stronger it becomes while he only becomes weaker, and its uprooting becomes more difficult.

Abu 'Uthman al-Maghribi

Know that this realm has an owner and that the sultan lives in the place of your being. Know yourself so that you will not be ashamed when you meet Him. Don't look down on anything; don't try to take someone else's share; know right from wrong, just from unjust—for the human being is built from the brick of lawful sustenance and the mortar of the advice of the wise.

Be conscious; take advice from what you see. Listen to your conscience, and talk with reason. Behave correctly even when you are by yourself. Kneel and sit low in the presence of the wise. Do not speak before being asked. If asked, be brief and say only that which you know. Know that the truth is with you always everywhere.

Speak gently to ignorance. Be polite and quiet in the presence of wisdom. If you ask of a teacher, ask with respect. Never ask a question with an intent to test. Accept the answer even if it is not what you expected.

Ibn 'Arabi

Khwaja Abdul-Karim said, "One day, a dervish asked me to write down some stories about my sheikh's miraculous powers. Shortly thereafter I received word that the sheikh wanted to see me. When I entered the sheikh's room, Abu Sa'id asked me what I was doing. I told him. He then advised me not to be a story-teller but to strive to reach the point where others would tell stories about me.

Abu Sa'id

If you want peace, calm your mind for ten minutes, for twenty minutes, for even five minutes. Do it with firmness, with absolute and complete faith, with certitude and determination to realize God and wisdom. When you have thought about this with your wisdom, say these two words in your heart, "*La ilaha,* other than You there is nothing, *ill-Allah,* only You are God." Say it and look at your heart.

If you intend this in your heart with faith, certitude, and determination, you can achieve peace of mind.

Bawa Muhaiyaddeen

A dervish was sweeping the courtyard. Abu Sa'id saw him and said, "Be like the dust ball that rolls before the broom and not like the rock left behind."

One must be like the dust, which has no will of its own but goes wherever the broom (the spiritual master) commands— not like the rock, which asserts its own will and resists the direction of the guide.

Abu Sa'id

Abu Sa'id had a newly initiated disciple by the name of Sankani, who came from a well-to-do family. He was young and enjoyed fine clothing and appearances. One day, Abu Sa'id was invited to an outing; a number of disciples, including Sankani, accompanied him. As they walked, Abu Sa'id noticed that Sankani seemed preoccupied with his own fine looks. The sheikh told Sankani not to walk in front of him. Sankani moved behind the sheikh. After a few minutes came the request, "Do not walk on my right." Sankani moved to the left, only to find that he was not supposed to be there either. He was perplexed, became upset, and asked the sheikh where he was supposed to be. Abu Sa'id then said, "I had been traveling for a while and regretted that I had not been able to attend the sheikh's sermons and enjoy lessons. When I came back to Mayhana and was again able to attend his sermons, he told me there would be no need to regret what I had missed even if I did not attend his lectures for ten years, because he always says only one thing, and that one thing can be written on a fingernail: 'Sacrifice your ego; nothing more.'"

Abu Sa'id

Pir asked Abu Sa'id whether he wanted to talk to God.

"Of course I want to."

"Then whenever you are by yourself, recite, 'Without Thee, O Beloved, I cannot rest; Thy goodness toward me I cannot reckon. Though every hair on my body becomes a tongue, a thousandth part of the thanks due to Thee I cannot tell.'"

Abu Sa'id

Our teachers accordingly have the habit of keeping accounts of what they said and what they did and recording everything in a notebook. After the evening prayer they would isolate themselves in their own homes so as to demand accounts of themselves. They would take up their notebook, examine their actions and words during the course of the day, and render to each of their actions whatever it deserved. If it merited the request for forgiveness, they requested forgiveness; if it merited repentance, they repented.

Ibn 'Arabi

Do everything you do in order to come close to your Lord in
your worship and prayers. Think that each deed may be your
last act, each prayer your last prostration, that you may not have
another chance. If you do this, it will be another motivation for
becoming heedful and also for becoming sincere and truthful.

Ibn 'Arabi

After this, he should close his eyes and think of himself as having died. They have stripped his corpse, laid it on the bench,
washed it and wrapped it in the shroud, prayed over it, and put
it to rest in the grave. He should reflect on each stage in this
process, for this meditation, which we call recollecting death, is
one of the practices of the Mystic Orders. To ponder one's death
is not to cause it, but it is harmful to avoid the thought of death.
For no one can or will escape the sure and destined end that
comes sooner or later to every mortal being. This meditation is
therefore an essential necessity for every lover of God.

Sheikh Muzaffer

Before the time of Prayer comes, the servant must be in a state
of preparation and his attitude must be that which is essential
for prayer, namely, a state of meditation and recollection, free
from wandering thoughts and consideration or remembrance of
anything save God alone. Those who enter in this way upon
prayer, with heart intent only upon God, will proceed from
prayer to prayer in that same state of recollection and will remain in that state after they have ceased to pray.

al-Sarraj

It is therefore a necessary prerequisite for lovers that they correct their lower selves by means of worship, spiritual exercises,
and Remembrance of God. Through these, the self may attain a

tranquil character, the heart be purified, and the spirit
burnished.

Sheikh Muzaffer

There are different levels of remembrance, and each has different ways. Some are expressed outwardly with audible voice,
some felt inwardly, silently, from the center of the heart. At the
beginning one should declare in words what one remembers.
Then stage by stage the remembrance spreads throughout one's
being—descending to the heart, then rising to the soul; then still
further it reaches the realm of the secrets; further to the hidden;
to the most hidden of the hidden. How far the remembrance
penetrates, the level it reaches, depends solely on the extent to
which Allah in His bounty has guided one.

Abdul Qadir al-Jilani

While performing the prayers of remembrance, put your hands
on your thighs, concentrate your heart, close your eyes, and
then, with total reverence, begin to utter the formula *La ilaha
illa 'llah* ["no god but God"] with all your might. Bring the
words *La ilaha* up from the navel, and direct the words *illa 'llah*
down to the heart in such a way that the effect and power of the
invocation reach all parts of the body. Do not raise your voice.
Keep it as hidden and as low as you can.

Meditate on the meaning in your heart. By *La ilaha* negate
any passing thought that may enter your heart. By doing so, you
say, in effect, "I desire nothing, seek nothing, and have no aim or
love 'but God' [*illa 'llah*]." Having negated all passing thoughts
with *La ilaha,* you affirm the Presence of Divine Majesty as your
only goal, purpose, and Beloved with *illa 'llah.*

Bawa Muhaiyaddeen

CHAPTER 14

Sufi Humor

One aspect of Sufi humor is the way in which it juxtaposes two views of life: one conventional and acceptable, the other a little out to the side, sometimes upside down. Often, it can open the floodgates of understanding more deftly than any other method. This "set-breaking" aspect is well understood within the Sufi tradition. Humor can be used as a tool to help us become more conscious of faults, to reveal that a relationship is deteriorating, to discover that a teacher is no longer serving us, or to realize that some culturally accepted rules of order, prudence, or education are deflecting our attention rather than focusing it on the path to awakening.

In most religious teachings, there is agreement that the human heart can be opened through prayer, suffering, wisdom, or love. These familiar ways have long and sometimes ponderous traditions associated with them. Humor as a catalyst to spiritual awareness is less well understood. Sufi teachers know, and use, the power of spontaneity and laughter, which can be at least as vital and powerful as any formal technique. The tradition of Sufism includes endless funny stories, usually on and about ourselves. For many of us, laughing at our faults is the first step in being able to release them.

One of the great bonuses in learning through humor is that even as you have a good time and doubt that you have learned anything, the lessons penetrate subtly, and stay with you, to come alive when the need arises.

This next section can be enjoyed without concern about its deeper meanings. If you wish, for example, you can imagine that these stories, all of which come from traditional Turkish story collections, are not about you. But if this were a teaching session, your task might be to identify yourself in every story, to acknowledge that you too could be as foolish or as lacking in discernment as the characters in these classic tales.

⤳

Hodja and his friends were sitting in a tea shop talking when a learned monk walked in and said pompously, "There is an answer for everything!"

Hodja responded, "Yet, I was approached by a rich and scholarly man with a question that I was not able to answer."

"Oh, if only I had been there!" boasted the monk. "Surely I would have answered it. Please tell it to me."

"Very well," Hodja replied, "this was the question: 'Why were you sneaking into my house through a window last night?'"

⤳

One day Hodja went to see his rich friend and said to him, "Please give me some money."

"But why?" asked the rich man.

"Well, I want to buy an elephant!" replied Hodja.

"If you have no money, how can you afford to keep an elephant?"

"I came here to get money, not advice," said Hodja.

⤳

One Friday Hodja stood up in the pulpit in the mosque to preach a sermon.

"O ye believers, do you know what I am going to talk about today?"

"We have no idea," they answered him.

"Well, if you have no idea at all, then what's the use of my talking to you?"

With that remark he descended from the pulpit and went home.

The next Friday he returned to the mosque and once again stood up in the pulpit and asked the congregation, "O ye true believers, do you know what I am going to talk about today?"

"Yes," they answered.

"Well, if you already know, then what's the use of my telling you?" And he again descended from the pulpit and went home.

Again the following Friday, he entered the mosque, mounted the pulpit, and asked the same question: "O ye true believers, do you know what I am going to talk to you about today?"

The congregation had prepared their answer in advance: "Some of us do, and some of us don't."

"In that case," Hodja said, "let those who know tell those who don't." And he went home again.

∽

"I can see in the dark," boasted Hodja one day while sitting in a tea shop.

"If that's true," said his friends, "why do we sometimes see you carrying a light at night?"

"Well," he replied, "I only use that lamp to prevent other people from bumping into me."

∽

One day a friend asked Hodja for a loan, saying that he would repay him the following week. Hodja didn't believe him but gave him the money anyway. Much to his surprise, the man kept his word and repaid him. A few months later the same man wanted another loan from Hodja, and he said to him, "You know my credit is good. Last time, I repaid you promptly."

"You're not going to get the money this time," said Hodja. "You deceived me last time by repaying me when I thought that you wouldn't. I am not going to let you fool me again."

〜

Hodja had become a very close friend to the king. His wise and humorous remarks made him one of the king's favorites.

One day the king was extremely hungry, so the palace chef prepared some eggplants. They were so delicious that the king told the chef to serve the dish every day.

"Is this not the very best vegetable in the world, Hodja?" he asked.

"Yes, your Majesty, the very best," he replied.

Five days later, after the same eggplant dish had been served for his fifth straight meal, the king roared: "Take this food away! It's awful."

"Yes, your Majesty. This is the worst vegetable in the world," said Hodja.

"But didn't you say only a few days ago that it was the best?"

"Yes, I did, your Majesty. But I am the servant of the king, not of the vegetable!"

〜

During one winter Hodja was having difficulty in getting by, so he started to think of ways to cut down his expenses. He decided to give his mule a little less barley. He did so, and the mule seemed content. A few days later he gave it a little less, and it still seemed to be happy. This continued until he was giving the animal less than half its normal ration. The mule moved more slowly and was quieter, but Hodja still thought it was healthy and happy. Then one morning, to his surprise, he entered his barn and found that his mule had died.

He wept and cried aloud: "Just when he was getting used to not eating."

⌣

Once Hodja was invited to a very important formal banquet, but he didn't dress up for the occasion and went in his everyday clothing. Once there he was treated with disrespect and was looked upon with contempt. No one paid him any attention; the servants ignored him and didn't even serve him dinner. After a short while he slipped out of the banquet unnoticed and went home. There he changed into his finest clothes, putting on a magnificent turban, a fine silk robe, very valuable jewelry, and a large, expensive overcoat. Then he returned to the banquet.

This time he was received with open arms. The host himself asked him to sit beside him at the highest seat and offered him a plate filled with the choicest delicacies. Much to their bewildered amazement, Hodja took off his coat, held it to the plate and said, "Eat, my master, eat."

"Hodja, what are you doing?" exclaimed his astonished host.

"It is the clothes that you are honoring, not me."

⌣

Hodja wanted to learn how to play the lute. So he approached a music teacher and asked him, "How much do you charge for private lute lessons?"

"Three silver pieces for the first month; then after that, one silver piece a month."

"Oh, that's very fair," exclaimed Hodja. "I'll start with the second month."

⌣

Hodja went to the market and bought a large sack full of potatoes. He put the sack on his shoulders, got on the donkey, and headed for home. But on the way he met some friends who said, "Hodja, it must be difficult for you to balance that sack with one hand and guide your donkey with the other. Why don't you tie the sack to the donkey?"

"The donkey has a big enough load to carry with me and doesn't need any extra weight, so I'm carrying the sack myself."

ᵔ

For some reason the people of Akshehir became very angry with Hodja and wanted to expel him from the town. They complained to the magistrate so that he was forced to summon Hodja. He said to him, "Hodja, the people of this town don't like you. They all want you to move."

"It is I who don't like the people here," replied Hodja. "As far as I'm concerned, they can all leave."

"But they are many and you are one," said the magistrate.

"Well, because they are many it is even easier for them. They can all work together and build a village wherever they decide to go. But how can I, all alone and at my age, build a new home and cultivate a field in the country?"

ᵔ

Hodja was riding on his donkey one day when it was frightened by something in its path and began to run very quickly. He couldn't manage to hold his donkey back, and some farmers yelled out, "Hodja, what's the hurry? Why are you going so fast?"

"Don't ask me," he shouted back. "Ask my donkey!"

ᵔ

A rich Persian came to Akshehir and began to boast about the tremendous palaces built in Isfahan by the shah, some of which, he said, had over two hundred rooms and covered thousands of square feet.

Hodja interrupted him by saying, "Ah, that's nothing! You should see the buildings that the sultan has built in our capital, Bursa. He has just built a hospital that is ten thousand feet long." Just then a man entered the room who had just returned from Bursa. "And a hundred feet wide!" continued Hodja.

"Well, that sounds like a most peculiar building. Why is the width not in proportion with its length?"

"It would have been," replied Hodja. "If my friend hadn't suddenly appeared."

〜

Once Hodja went hunting and managed to catch a few quail. He plucked and roasted them and then put them in a large pot, put the lid on, and went off to invite some friends over for dinner. While he was out, someone came and took out the roasted quail and put live ones in their place.

Hodja came back with his friends a little while later and proudly took the lid off the pot. Immediately all the quail flew out of the window and disappeared from sight. Hodja was in a state of shock. When he recovered, he said, "Oh my God! That was truly a miracle indeed! Dear Lord, I believe that only you can bring the dead back to life. But, if I may ask, what happened to the butter, salt, pepper, and all those spices?"

〜

One day a poor hungry man was passing through the streets with only a piece of bread in his hand. As he passed by a restaurant, he saw some delicious-looking meatballs frying in a pan. He waved his bread over the pan for a few seconds, and then he ate it. The restaurant owner had seen what he did and grabbed him by the neck and dragged him before the judge, who happened to be Hodja. The restaurant owner demanded that this poor peasant pay for the price of the meatballs.

Hodja listened carefully and then took two coins from his pocket and told him, "Come and stand by me a minute." The restaurant owner obeyed, and Hodja shook his fist so that the coins made a rattling sound in the man's ear.

"What are you doing this for?" he asked.

Hodja replied, "I have just paid you for the meatballs. Surely the sound of money is fair payment for the smell of food."

⤺

One day Hodja was heartbroken over the loss of his dear wife. All his neighbors and friends tried to encourage and comfort him by saying, "Don't worry about her, Hodja, we'll help you to find an even better one."

A short while later his donkey died as well. Hodja seemed to mourn the donkey even more than he had his wife. Some of his friends noticed this and approached him concerning this matter, and he replied, "When my wife passed away, all my friends promised me that they would find an even better one for me, but so far no one has offered to replace my donkey."

⤺

At midnight Hodja heard of a lot of commotion outside his window. He wrapped his blanket around himself and went outside to see what was happening. He saw two men fighting and tried to break it up. Without answering, one of them ripped the blanket off him, and both of them quickly ran away. So poor Hodja walked back into his house naked and returned to his bed.

"What was the fighting all about?" asked his wife.

"It was over our blanket. Now that they have got it, they have stopped fighting."

⤺

One day a friend visited Hodja and said, "Hodja, I want to borrow your donkey."

"I'm sorry," replied Hodja, "but I've already lent it out to someone else."

As soon as he said this, the donkey brayed.

"But Hodja, I can hear the donkey! It's in the stable."

Shutting the door in this friend's face, Hodja told him with dignity, "A man who believes the word of a donkey above my own doesn't deserve to be lent anything!"

⤺

All the men in the tea shop were criticizing a certain man named Abdul. They all said that he was just a good-for-nothing vagabond.

One of the leading men of the town said, "That man is a cabbage."

Everyone nodded in agreement except Hodja. "That's not true, my friend. A cabbage can at least be cooked and eaten and used by the body. But of what use is Abdul?"

⤺

Once, in a tea shop, some soldiers were boasting about a few of their recent victories. The local people were gathered around them, listening eagerly.

"And I took my double-edged sword and charged the enemy fearlessly," said one.

Then there was a loud round of applause.

"Oh, that reminds me," remarked Hodja, "of the time I cut the leg off an enemy on the battlefield. I cut it right off!"

"Sir, it would have been better," replied the captain of the soldiers, "to have cut off his head."

"Of course, I would have. But somebody else had already done that."

⤺

One day the king sent for Hodja and asked him to go bear hunting. Hodja was terrified of the idea, but he had to go nevertheless.

When he got back to the village, somebody asked him, "How did the hunt go?"

"Just wonderful," he replied.

"How many bears did you kill?"

"None."

"How many did you chase?"

"None."

"How many did you see?"

"None."

"Well, how was it 'just wonderful' then?"

"Because," Hodja replied, "when you are hunting bears, 'none' is more than enough."

CHAPTER 15

Virtues

FAITH

Faith is something easy to speak of, but difficult to practice. We often place our faith in everything but God. We have faith in our lawyers when there is legal trouble and place even greater faith in our doctors when we are sick. We have faith that our money will protect us, faith that our own intelligence will save us from difficulties. That is, we seem to have faith in creation, but not in our Creator.

One of the Ninety-nine Attributes of God is ya Salaam, or Peace. Salaam also means safety, security, and health, wholeness. If you lean against a rotten tree trunk, it will not support you. You can rely only on that which is truly healthy and whole, and that is God. Nothing else provides completely trustworthy support and security. And so, the only real peace comes from faith in God.

Our faith is often tested. God, who is all-knowing, already comprehends the outcome. God tests us so that we can better know ourselves. The following could easily have been a Sufi story:

A man fell off a cliff and barely managed to catch hold of a small bush. There was a great drop below him, and the top of the cliff was too far to reach. To make matters worse, the bush began slowly coming loose. At this moment, the man realized that he could rely on nothing but God. With his momentary perfect faith, he called upon God for help. A heavenly voice answered, "Let go of the bush!" Silent for a moment, the man cried out, "Is there anyone else up there I could talk to?"

By reading the words of those who did have real faith, perhaps we will begin to understand what faith is and how to develop it.

✑

A wealthy man went to his garden, where his eye fell upon the beautiful wife of his gardener. He sent the man away and said to the woman, "Shut the gates." She replied, "I have shut them all except one, which I cannot shut." He asked, "Which one is that?" "The gate," said she, "that is between us and God." On receiving this answer, the man repented and begged to be forgiven.

Jami

To completely trust in God is to be like a child who knows deeply that even if he does not call for the mother, the mother is totally aware of his condition and is looking after him.

al-Ghazzali

The disciples of Abu al-Bistami once complained to him about the Devil. They said, "The Devil takes away our faith." The sheikh then summoned the Devil and questioned him. The Devil said, "I cannot force anyone to do anything. I fear God too much to dare to try that. Actually, most people throw their faith away for all sorts of trivial reasons. I simply pick up the faith they throw away.

Sheikh Muzaffer

Once Hasan al-Basri, accompanied by several people, was on the way to Mecca. They came to a well. They were all thirsty but had no rope to pull up a bucket of water. Hasan said, "I am going to pray. While I am praying you will see the water rise. Drink freely and quench your thirst."

So it happened. But when one man, after drinking, filled his water bag for future use, the water sank to its original level. When asked the reason for the strange occurrence, Hasan replied, "It was due to your lack of faith to depend solely on God."

Attar

Ibrahim Adham said, "Faith in God will be firmly established if three veils are cast aside:

1. "feeling pleasure in possessing anything;
2. "lamenting over the loss of anything;
3. "enjoying self-praise."

al-Ghazzali

Once, Hasan al-Basri was partaking of the meager meal prepared by poor al-'Ajami when a beggar knocked at the door. Al-'Ajami took all the food he had prepared and gave it to the beggar. Surprised at this strange behavior, Hasan said, "You must know little of manners." Al-'Ajami remained silent. Then a lady appeared bearing plates of delicious food. Both men sat and ate. Then al-'Ajami said, "Hasan, you are a good man. You should develop a little more faith in God and remember that anything given in God's name returns severalfold."

Attar

No one ever suffered on the path of faith who did not find the remedy for his or her pain.

Jami

Some people saw Caliph Omar quicken his pace as he passed by a wall that was about to collapse. "O Omar," they asked, "are you running from destiny?" "No," he replied, "I am taking refuge with destiny from destiny!"

Sheikh Muzaffer

HUMILITY

Humility might be defined as "taking one's true measure" and then not hiding from the truth of that realization. Humility, Sufis aver, is a state that is achieved, not through practice, but through awareness.

Benjamin Franklin, at one point in his life, made it a practice to work on one virtue each week. He was making excellent progress, he felt, in his self-development until he worked on humility. What he found was that, as often as he practiced, and made himself more conscious of humility in his life, the prouder he became of his own progress.

What then is your true measure? In the context of this world, you are one among billions, here for but a single breath. You matter to very few people, and even the few who know you may think about you seldom.

Without humility, we can be as puffed up about ourselves as the gnat in the following story: A self-important gnat, having raised his family for some years in the ear of an elephant, finally decided to move. Shouting at the top of his tiny lungs, he informed the elephant of what was, to him, a momentous decision. The elephant, having previously known nothing of the gnat's existence, made no reply, not wishing to hurt the feelings of his small and totally insignificant visitor.

Even if you see yourself as a part of all creation and lasting for eternity, you, as a single human, are still but a drop in a vast ocean. That ocean is held by gravity to a small sphere orbiting a tiny star among billions of others. Your time as a separate drop, however important you may seem to be in your own world, is so brief that the ocean itself may be unaware of your existence, your forming, or your dissolving.

Somebody once hit Bayazid Bistami with a stick. The stick broke. The venerable saint took a new stick and a bowl of honey and gave them to the man who had struck him, saying, "Because of my face, your stick broke and you suffered loss, so here is a new one in its place and some honey for you to eat."

Sheikh Muzaffer

One day in Baghdad the central bazaar caught on fire. Someone came to me and told me that my store had been spared in the fire. I replied, "Praise be to God!" At that moment, I became ashamed before people for selfishly seeking my own advantage. Thirty years now I've been asking God to forgive me for once saying that "Praise be to God."

Sari

"All my brothers are better than I!"

"How is that?"

"Every one of them considers me more worthy than himself, and whoever rates me higher than himself is in fact better than I."

al-Ghazzali

One day a man came to the teacher Bayazid and said, "I have fasted and prayed for thirty years and have found none of the spiritual joy of which you speak."

"If you had fasted and prayed for three hundred years, you would never find it," answered the sage.

"How is that?" asked the man.

"Your selfishness is acting as a veil between you and God."

"Tell me the cure."

"It is a cure you cannot carry out," said Bayazid.

Those around him pressed him to reveal it. After a time he spoke: "Go to the nearest barbershop and have your head shaved; strip yourself of your clothes except for a loincloth. Take a nosebag full of walnuts, hang it around your neck. Go into the market and cry out—'Anybody who gives me a slap on the neck shall have a walnut.' Then proceed to the law courts and do the same thing."

"I can't do that," said the man. "Suggest some other remedy."

"This is the indispensable preliminary to a cure," answered Bayazid. "But as I told you, you are incurable."

al-Ghazzali

One day on the bank of the River Dajla, Hasan saw a man seated with a young lady and a bottle of wine in front of him. A thought crossed his mind, "How depraved is this man! How unlike me." Just then a boat appeared in the river a little distance from them and gradually began to sink in the deep water. That man immediately jumped into the water and swam toward the seven men in the boat who were drowning. He saved six and then, looking toward Hasan, said, "If you are superior to me, then in God's name save the seventh man."

Hasan did so. The man then said to Hasan, "Sir, this woman seated by my side is my mother, and this bottle contains only water. All this was enacted to put you to the test." Hasan fell on his knees and said, "Just as you saved those six people, save me as well. I am drowning in the waters of pride and vanity." The man replied, "May God fulfill your desire!"

Attar

Spurred with the desire to gain publicity for himself, one day Hasan, seeing Rabia in a general congregation of saints, came to her and said, "Rabia, let us leave this congregation and, sitting on the waters of the lake, hold our spiritual discussion there." He said this to display his miraculous power before others, for he had gained mastery over water as Christ had walked over water.

Rabia remonstrated, "Hasan, put your vanity aside. If you are so determined to separate yourself from the general assembly of saints, why should we not both fly and hold our meeting in the air?" Rabia said this as if she had that power. Hasan knew he could not do this and said as much, shamed by her words.

Rabia said, "Know that what you can do fishes can also do—easily. What I suggested was no more than what a fly does. Reality transcends this miracle-mongering. Seek humility."

Attar

To be a dervish means to be a lump of sifted earth
with a little water sprinkled on top.
It means to be something that
neither harms the soles of the feet
nor leaves a trail of dust behind.

Ansari

The Sufi becomes more humble every hour, for every hour is drawing him nearer to God. The Sufis see without knowledge, without sight, without information received, and without observation, without description, without veiling, and without veil. They are not themselves, but insofar as they exist at all, they exist in God. Their movements are caused by God, and their words are the words of God uttered by their tongues, and their sight is the sight of God, which has entered into their eyes. So God Most High has said, "When I love a servant, I, the Lord, am his ear so that he hears by Me; I am his eye so that he sees by Me; and I am his tongue so that he speaks by Me; and I am his hand so that he takes by Me."

Ibn 'Arabi

I am fully qualified to work as a doorkeeper, for this reason: What is inside me, I don't let out; what is outside me, I don't let in. If someone comes in, he goes right out again. He has nothing to do with me at all. I am a Doorkeeper of the Heart, not a lump of wet clay.

Rabia

GRATITUDE

Gratitude transforms us. It opens our hearts and brings us closer to God. Unfortunately most of us are unconscious of the many blessings we receive and rarely feel gratitude. Or if we do feel gratitude, it is often extremely short-lived.

I have been amazed by observing older dervishes serve one another. Even when serving a glass of water or a cup of tea, the one who is serving is attentive and grateful for the chance to serve. The dervish who is served receives whatever is served with real gratitude, as opposed to taking it for granted. This is all done quietly, with no outer show or fanfare.

For months after a serious car accident, I would wake up each morning in great pain. I would look out my bedroom window into my garden and weep—with gratitude. I was alive, and this world was filled with beauty.

The prophet Muhammad said, "Gratitude for the abundance you have received is the best insurance that the abundance will continue." There is another old saying, "Count your blessings." There is more truth in it than we generally realize.

Whoever is content with the gift and does not see the Giver, his heart is attentive only to the gift and neglectful of the Giver.

Baba Taher

Whoever does not express his gratitude to people will never be able to be grateful to God.

Muhammad

The Sufi is pleased with all that God does in order that God may be pleased with all that he does.

Abu Sa'id

Sultan Mahmud of Ghazna once shared a cucumber with Ayaz, his favorite courtier. The sultan peeled the cucumber, and then gave half of it to Ayaz with his own hand and ate the other half himself. The sultan noticed that the cucumber he was eating was as bitter as poison, but Ayaz seemed to be enjoying his half, so he asked him in surprise, "How is it that you are not even screwing up your face, when the cucumber you're eating is so bitter? Why don't you spit it out?"

Ayaz replied, "My dear sultan, I have enjoyed so many favors from your hands. After all that, how could the cucumber taste bitter? Would it not be ungrateful of me to spit out what you have given me now? Even if you did give me something bitter, it would taste sweet to me."

Sheikh Muzaffer

A Sufi visited a foreign sheikh and asked him about real Sufism as taught in his country. The sheikh replied that, when God sent them something, they would eat it and be grateful, if not, they would practice patience. The visitor replied, "That kind of Sufism is what our dogs do at home—when they find a bone they eat it; otherwise they are patient until they are fed." The sheikh then asked how *he* would define Sufism. The visitor answered, "When we have anything, we give it away, and if we have nothing, we occupy ourselves with thanks and pray for forgiveness."

Sheikh Muzaffer

We are by nature astonishingly heedless and incapable of gratitude. We can spend a whole lifetime enjoying various benefits and not appreciate their value until we are deprived of them. How many lovers boldly contemplate separation, fondly imagining that they have had enough of the beloved. And yet as soon as they actually experience separation, they burn up with longing.

Jami

Sofyan cried out in Rabia's presence, "O God! that You might be content with me!" Rabia reproached him, saying, "Aren't you ashamed to ask God to be content with you when you are not content with God?" To this Sofyan exclaimed, "God forgive me!"

Abu Makki

Jafar asked Rabia when a devotee might become content with God. She replied, "When his joy in affliction equals his joy in blessing."

Abu Makki

Ibn al-Masak went to the caliph, who at the time was drinking a cup of water. The caliph requested al-Masak to instruct him. Al-Masak said, "If you were dying with thirst and a cup of water was offered to you in exchange for your kingdom, you would gladly accept the bargain, wouldn't you?" The caliph agreed. "Then why are you proud of a kingdom that is not worth more than a drink of water, and why aren't you grateful to the Lord for having supplied you with so much water free?"

al-Ghazzali

If someone gave you a beautiful, expensive new hat, wouldn't you be grateful for the generous gift? But shouldn't you be even more grateful to the One who gave you the *head* to put that hat on?

Sheikh Muzaffer

POVERTY

The poet Gary Snyder says, "The truly affluent are those who do not need anything." That observation does not refer to your material wealth, but speaks about the condition of your heart.

Though many Sufi saints have owned little or no property, this was a matter of choice, not of necessity. True wealth is a state in which you do not crave anything that you do not already have.

What the Sufis mean by "poverty" is lack of attachment to anything but air, food, and sleep. A heart that is full of the things of this world has no place for God. An empty heart has space to long for God to fill it.

There was a poor fisherman who was a Sufi teacher. He went fishing every day, and each day he would distribute his catch to the poor of his village, except for a fish head or two that he used to make soup for himself. His students dearly loved and admired their "fish-head sheikh."

One of the students was a merchant. Before traveling to Cordoba, the teacher asked him to convey his greetings to his own teacher, the great sage Ibn 'Arabi, and to ask the sage for some advice to help him in his own spiritual work, which he felt was going very slowly.

When the merchant arrived at Ibn 'Arabi's house, he found, much to his surprise, a veritable palace surrounded by elaborate gardens. He saw many servants going back and forth and was served a sumptuous meal on gold plates by beautiful young women and handsome young men. Finally he was brought to Ibn 'Arabi, who was wearing clothing fit for a sultan. He conveyed his teacher's greetings and repeated his teacher's request for spiritual guidance. Ibn 'Arabi said simply, "Tell my student that he is too worldly!" The merchant was shocked and offended by this advice coming from someone living in such worldly opulence.

When he returned, his teacher immediately asked about his meeting with Ibn 'Arabi. The merchant repeated Ibn 'Arabi's words and added that this sounded totally absurd coming from such a wealthy, worldly man.

His teacher replied, "You should know that each of us can have as much material wealth as his soul can handle without losing sight of God. What you saw in him was not merely material wealth but great spiritual attainment." Then the teacher added, with tears in his eye, "Besides, he is right. Often at night as I make my simple fish-head soup, I wish it were an entire fish!"

All that you need from the world is something lawful to satisfy your hunger, something with which to cover yourself, and a roof over your head. Let these be the only things you ask from this world.

Ibn 'Arabi

HOME EQUITY
God's hands over my head—
that's what a roof means!
But when I wake up in Spring light,
the only thing of worth is an open door.

John Fox

To become a saint of God, you must covet nothing in this world or the next and you must give yourself entirely to God and turn your face to Him. To desire this world is turning away from God for the sake of what is transitory. To covet the next world means turning away from God for the sake of what is everlasting.

Ibrahim Adham

The highest asceticism was displayed by Christ when he threw away the brick he used as a pillow after the devil asked him why he kept it if he had renounced the world.

al-Ghazzali

A certain man was constantly bewailing his poverty. Ibrahim Adham said to him. "My son, perhaps you paid little for your poverty." "You are talking nonsense," said the man. "You should be ashamed of yourself. Does anyone buy poverty?"

Ibrahim replied, "For my part I chose it of my own free will; moreover, I bought it at the price of this world's sovereignty and gave up my kingdom and my ruling over others. I would buy one instant of this poverty again with a hundred worlds, for every moment it becomes worth more to me. When I found this precious merchandise, I gave my final farewells to royalty. Without any doubt I know the value of poverty. While you remain in ignorance of it, I give thanks for it."

Ibrahim Adham

One day Abu Muhammad went to visit his friend Shiekh Abu Sa'id at the public bathhouse. When he found him he asked, "Is the bathhouse pleasant?"

"It certainly is."

"Why do you think so?"

"Because you have graced this place with your presence."

"I'm afraid that is not a good reason."

"Would you honor me by giving me the reason?"

"This place is pleasant because one needs no more than a jug of water to pour water on one's body and a towel to dry oneself with, and these items belong not to the bather but to the bath keeper."

Abu Sa'id

PATIENCE

Patience is one of the Ninety-nine Names of Divine Attributes mentioned in the Koran. It is one of the most frequently mentioned Attributes in the Koran.

It is said that patience is half of faith. Patience is a spiritual state. It is a real accomplishment and one that is not easy to attain.

Without patience we can do nothing well; with patience, difficult tasks become easy. If we are impatient, we are no longer in the present; we are busy wishing for a future that has not yet come. We have all had times of patience, peak experiences in which we have fully enjoyed the present moment, with no thought of the future. To observe real patience in action, watch a master at any skill. Master potters, artists, or musicians live in the present. Their skill demands present-centered patience.

For most of us, our lives would be greatly enhanced by greater patience—professionally, personally, and spiritually.

The great Sufi saint and philosopher Ibn 'Arabi was asked by his teacher to explain the meaning of the verse from the Koran "I require no provision from them, nor do I need them to feed Me." Ibn 'Arabi thought for a while and then left without a word. Four years later, when he returned to his sheikh, the first thing his teacher said was, "Give me your answer. After four years, the time is ripe for it."

Ibn 'Arabi

Contentment is the putting aside of free will.

Junaid

One day, Sari was asked about patience. He spoke on the subject with words full of wisdom. As he was speaking, a scorpion stung his foot repeatedly, but Sari did not interrupt his talk.

When people became aware of the situation and asked him why he had not moved his foot away from the scorpion, he replied, "I was discussing patience; I could hardly give you counsel and advice on that subject without being patient myself. I would have been ashamed before God."

Sheikh Muzaffer

Patience has three stages. First, the servant ceases to complain; this is the stage of repentance. Second, the Sufi becomes satisfied with what is decreed; this is the rank of the ascetic. Third, the servant comes to love whatever the Lord does with him; this is the stage of the true friends of God.

Abu Talib al-Makki

Khafif went out on a pilgrimage and carried only a jug and a rope to draw water. As he passed through the wilderness, he saw many deer standing on the top of a well, drinking water. As he approached, they ran away, and the level of the water went down. In spite of his efforts, he could not draw water from the well. He prayed to the Lord to raise the level of the water as He had done for the deer. The Divine Voice replied, "We cannot do so, as you depend upon the rope and the jug besides Us." Immediately he threw both of them away and the water level rose and he quenched his thirst.

He recited the incident to Junaid, who said, "The Lord was testing your dependence on Him. Had you waited patiently for a longer time, it would have overflowed the top."

Attar

GENEROSITY

If everything flows from God and everything returns to God, do you truly own anything? Are you not but a steward, taking care of that the portion of this world under your care, which is to be preserved and protected and possibly shared?

There are different forms of generosity. Most of us feel generous when we give something—money, time, advice. We know that our generosity is successful when we are seen, acknowledged, thanked, and praised for what we have done. This is the most obvious level of generosity. The truth of the matter is, in these cases, we give and we are repaid. These transactions are actually exchanges and contain little actual generosity.

A higher level of generosity is to give anonymously. The giver still benefits, but not as directly. Payment comes from knowing that we have been not only generous but also virtuous in not expecting to gain recognition for our giving. However, the recipient will still feel gratitude, and inside ourselves, we assure ourselves, intuitively, that we gain merit.

The Sufis speak of still another level—"secret charity." This occurs when you give so that someone benefits from your actions, but unlike at the other two levels, that person does not feel given to, nor is there any burden of gratitude. How do you feel, for example, if you find a dollar bill on the sidewalk? You look around and pick it up with a smile on your face. You may feel blessed, or at least lucky. You don't feel that someone "gave it to you" but that you found it. If, however, someone made a practice of laying bills on the ground now and then—then walking away and telling no one—he or she would be practicing a simple form of secret charity.

If you try something like this, you will soon feel the effects in your life. If you look for small, daily opportunities, they abound. My library, for example, has a place where I can donate books so I can get a tax deduction. They also have a box so that books can be given anonymously. The choice is mine.

You can practice generosity with other than things. It is possible to give your time, your knowledge, your labor, and your skills. Having little money is no excuse for a lack of generosity.

At yet another level, if you give what is in your heart—patience, insight, compassion—you will find not only that your generosity arises from God, but that each act of giving also becomes an act of remembrance.

Two brothers, one married and one single, farmed together and divided the grain from the harvest equally between them. The single brother often thought that his brother had extra worries and expenses because of his family so he would, from time to time, move some of the filled sacks from his storeroom into his brother's. His brother, on the other hand, often thought of how lonely his single brother must be. He thought, if my brother had a little more money he might buy himself some nicer things. So he would, without the other's knowledge, move some of his grain sacks into his brother's storeroom.

For many years the number of sacks remained equal between them, and neither brother could ever understand why this was so.

Traditional

They are true men of generosity who, having escaped from self, sit huddled in the corner of selflessness. Freed from the bondage of nature and the snares of greed, they are as dust on the road of suffering and love. No human heart is ever clouded because of them; nor do men impose any burden upon them. They harmonize the discords of this world and patiently bear whatever befalls them. They sleep in peace each night, devoid of any hatred or strife; and they arise each dawn in the same state as they retired.

Jami

Prayers for the dead are on the same footing as gifts for the living. The angel goes in to the dead with a tray of light, bearing a cloth of light, and says, "This is a gift for you from your brother so-and-so, from your relative so-and-so." And he delights in it just as a living person rejoices in a gift.

al-Ghazzali

One day Mulla Nasruddin saw a crowd gathered around a pond. A Muslim priest with a huge turban on his head had fallen in the water and was calling for help. People were leaning over and saying, "Give me your hand, Reverend! Give me your hand!" But the priest didn't pay attention to their offer to rescue him; he kept wrestling with the water and shouting for help.

Finally the Mulla stepped forward. "Let me handle this." He stretched out his hand toward the priest and shouted at him, "Take my hand!"

The priest grabbed the Mulla's hand and was hoisted out of the pond. People, very surprised, asked the Mulla for the secret of his strategy.

"It is very simple," he replied. "I knew this miser wouldn't give anything to anyone. So instead of saying, 'Give me your hand,' I said, 'Take my hand,' and sure enough he took it."

Rumi

A miser hoarded all his wealth and spent nothing on his family.
But one day his son discovered the hiding place. He dug up all
the gold and put a large stone in its place. The money, he spent
in riotous living. His father soon discovered his loss and was
overcome with grief, but his son said cheerfully, "Gold is for
spending, father. For hiding, a stone is just as good."

Sa'di

The people of Baghdad asked Junaid to tell them the meaning of
generosity. He said, "I will hear another define it first."

"Generosity is not identifying with yourself, and acting as
well as possible," said Hasan. The people applauded his wisdom.

Junaid commented, "Hasan has spoken well, but he has not
emptied the cup. I feel that generosity is doing justice without
requiring justice."

Hasan said to the others. "I shall sit at Junaid's feet, for I
spoke only about mankind. His speech is from a divine source."

Junaid

Sheba sent a gift of forty loads of gold to Solomon. When she
reached the land of Solomon, she saw that the mountains and
field, even the dust in the road, were pure gold. Day after day she
rode on gold until gold lost all value for her. When Solomon saw
her gift, he laughed. "When did I ever ask for porridge from
you? I did not ask for gifts; I asked that you be worthy of those
gifts I will give you."

Rumi

A student said to his teacher, "What am I to do? I am troubled
by the people, many of whom make me visits. By their coming
and going they encroach upon my precious time." The teacher
replied, "Lend something to every one of them who is poor and
ask something from everyone of them who is rich, and they will
come round thee no more."

Sa'di

Spend from what Allah has given you. Do not fear poverty. Allah will give you what He has promised, whether you or everyone asks for it or does not ask for it. No one who has been generous has ever perished in destitution.

Ibn 'Arabi

It is said that one night a thief entered Junaid's house but found nothing to steal except a shirt, which he took. The next day, Junaid passed through the bazaar and saw his shirt being sold by an auctioneer. The prospective buyer was insisting that someone be provided who would testify that the seller really owned the shirt. Junaid stepped up and said, "I am ready to testify that it is his."

Junaid

There was a man who had heartlessly murdered ninety-nine people. Then, he felt remorse. He went to a learned man and told him about his past, explaining that he wished to repent, reform, and become a better person. "I wonder if Allah will pardon me?" he asked. For all his learning, the scholar was a man who had not been able to digest what he had learned. "You will not be pardoned," he said. "Then I may as well kill you, too," said the other. And kill him he did. He then found another worthy individual and told him that he had killed a hundred people. "I wonder," he said, "whether Allah will pardon me if I repent?" Being a truly wise man, he replied, "Of course you will be pardoned; repent at once. I have just one piece of advice for you: avoid the company of wicked men and mix with good people, for bad company leads one into sin." The man expressed repentance and regret, weeping as he sincerely implored his Lord to pardon him. Then, turning his back on bad company, he set off to find a neighborhood where righteous people lived. On the way, his appointed hour arrived, and he died. The angels of punishment and of mercy both came to take away his soul. The angels of punishment said that as a sinful person he rightfully belonged to them, but the angels of mercy also claimed him, saying, "He repented and had resolved to become a good man. He was on his way to a place where righteous people live, but his appointed hour had come." A great debate ensued, and Gabriel was sent as an arbitrator to settle this affair. After hearing both sides he gave this verdict: "Measure the ground. If the spot where he died is closer to the good people, then he belongs to the angels of mercy, but if it is nearer to the wicked people, he will be given to the angels of punishment." They measured the ground. Because the man had just set out, he was still closer to the wicked. But because he has been sincere in his repentance, the Lord moved the spot where he lay and brought it to just outside the city of the good people. That penitent servant was handed over to the angels of mercy.

Sheikh Muzaffer

Harun al-Rashid was once walking through a plantation when he saw a hunched old graybeard putting in sapling date palms. He greeted him, saying, "Take it easy, father!"

"Thank you, my son," the old man replied.

"What are you doing, father?" asked the caliph.

"As you see, I am planting sapling date palms."

"How many years does it take a date palm to bear fruit?"

"Ten, twenty, thirty years. Some take as long as a hundred years."

"Will you be able to eat the fruit of these palms you are planting?"

"I may not live to see the day," said the old man, "but we eat from those our forebears planted. So let us plant, that those who follow us may eat in turn!" His words impressed the caliph, who tossed him a purse of money. The old man took the gold pieces, saying, "I give praise to Allah, for the saplings I planted have borne fruit immediately!" The caliph was pleased to hear him say this, and he gave him another purse of gold.

Said the old man, "I give praise to Allah, for trees normally bear fruit only once a year, but mine have produced two crops in one year!"

Throwing him yet another purse of gold, the caliph turned to the servant at his side and said, "Quick, let us get away from here before this old man leaves us penniless."

Sheikh Muzaffer

A man once wished to give some money to the venerable Ibrahim Adham. The saint said to him, "If you are rich I shall accept your money, but if you are bankrupt I shall not take it."

"I am rich," the would-be giver assured him, whereupon the following conversation took place between them:

"So you are rich, are you; how much money do you have?"

"I have two thousand gold pieces."

"Do you wish to have four thousand?"

"Of course, I do."

"Wouldn't you rather have eight thousand?"

"Naturally."

"Would you be happier if you had ten thousand gold pieces?"

"No doubt about it."

"You say you are rich, but you are nothing of the sort. You are an impoverished bankrupt from whom I do not accept money. Keep the money you wanted to give me, add to it the rest, and go on your way, happy."

Sheikh Muzaffer

Abu 'Abd Allah al-Khayat had a tailor shop in which he would sit and a Zoroastrian client who made use of his services. Whenever he made something for this Zoroastrian, the latter would pay him with false coins, which Abu 'Abd Allah would take, without either saying anything to him or refusing them. Now, it so fell out that one day Abu 'Abd Allah had left his shop on some task, and the Zoroastrian came, and, not finding him, paid his apprentice instead—with a bad coin. The apprentice looked at it, saw that it was bad, and gave it back. When Abu 'Abd Allah returned, he told him what had occurred. "You have done wrong!" Abu 'Abd Allah said. "The Zoroastrian has been dealing with me in this fashion for some while, and I have been patient with him, taking his coins and throwing them into a well so that no other Muslim might be taken by them."

al-Khayat

Abu Sulayman al-Darani used to say: "If I owned the whole world to put in the mouth of a brother of mine, I would still deem it too little for him."

He also said, "I feed a morsel to a brother of mine and find the taste of it in my own throat."

al-Ghazzali

In sharing one's property with one's companion there are three degrees.

The lowest degree is where you place your companion on the same footing as your slave or your servant, attending to his or her need from your surplus. If some need befalls him when you have more than you require, you give spontaneously, not obliging him to ask. To oblige your companion to ask is the ultimate shortcoming in fulfilling one's duty.

At the second degree you place your companion on the same footing as yourself. You are content to have him or her as partner in your property and to treat him or her like yourself, to the point of sharing it equally.

At the third degree, the highest of all, you prefer your companion to yourself and set his or her need before your own.

al-Ghazzali

Some Israelites insulted Jesus one day as he walk through the marketplace.

He answered them only by repeating prayers in their name.

Someone said to him, "You prayed for these men. Do you not feel anger at their treatment of you?"

He answered, "I could spend only what I carry in my purse."

Attar

PART 6

In Touch with the Divine

CHAPTER 16

How to Know God

The goal of all mystical experience is to know God. Sufism provides us with a variety of means, including service, love, and self-discipline.

The paths to God are as numerous as there are seekers. And yet all these paths have common elements, as we are more alike than we are different.

The more motivated we are, the more effort we tend to devote to the goal, and the more likely we are to succeed. Do we really want to know God? How badly? How much are we willing to do in order to attain the goal?

As one modern teacher, Sheikh Tosun Bayrak, has said, "If the search for God is not the most important thing in your life, you are not ready to join us."

⌒

One day a man asked a sheikh how to reach God. "The ways to God," the sheikh replied, "are as many as there are created

beings. But the shortest and easiest is to serve others, not to
bother others, and to make others happy."

Abu Sa'id

O seeker, know that the path to Truth is within you. You are the
traveler. Going happens by itself. Coming happens to you, without you. There is no arriving or leaving; nor is there any place;
nor is there a contained within a container. Who is there to be
with God? What is there other than God? Who seeks and finds
when there is none but God?

Sheikh Badruddin

There is great wisdom in acting for God's sake and refusing to
act for any other reason. Once Ali, the son-in-law of the Prophet,
was fighting on the battlefield with one of the most powerful
champions of the enemy. He finally managed to strike the warrior's sword from his hand. As he raised his sword to take the
enemy's life, the man spat in Ali's face. Ali stopped and sheathed
his sword. The warrior said, "I don't understand. You were about
to kill me, and yet after I spit at you, you spare my life. Why?"

Ali replied, "I was going to take your life in battling for God's
sake, but when you spat at me, it angered me. Had I killed you
then, I would have been a murderer, for I would have struck in
anger. I will fight for God, but I will not murder for my ego."

Sheikh Muzaffer

Adam was still a child, so God brought him into the path of ca-
resses. The path of children is one thing, the furnace of heroes
something else. Adam was taken into Paradise on the shoulders
of the great angels of God's kingdom. Paradise was made the
cradle for his greatness and the pillow for his leadership, because
he still did not have the endurance for the court of severity. . . .

Tomorrow, Adam will go into Paradise with his children. A
cry will rise up from all the particles of Paradise because of the

crowding. The angels of the world of the dominion will look with wonder and say, "Is this that same man who moved out of Paradise a few days ago in poverty and indigence?" Suffer a bit of trouble, then in a few days, take the treasure!

Samani

The prophet Abraham grew up among idol worshipers. He sought to find God. He looked at the brightest stars and said, "You are my Lord." Then the full moon came out. It was far bigger and brighter than any of the stars. Abraham looked at the moon and said, "You are my Lord." Then the sun came up, and the moon and stars disappeared. Abraham said, "You are the greatest, You are my Lord." Then night came, and the sun disappeared.

Abraham said, "My Lord is the One who changes things and who brings them back. My Lord is the One who is behind all changes."

Sheikh Muzaffer

For one moment sink into the ocean of God, and do not suppose that one hair of your head shall be moistened by the water of the seven seas. If the vision you behold is the Face of God, there is no doubt that from this time forward you will see clearly. When the foundations of your own existence are destroyed, have no fear in your heart that you yourself will perish.

Hafiz

It is said that when you take only one step toward Him, He advances ten steps toward you. But the complete truth is that God is always with you.

Muhammad

You've been walking in circles,
searching.

Don't drink by the water's edge.
Throw yourself in. Become the water.
Only then will your thirst end.

Jeanette Berson

The end reached by the theologian is the beginning of the way
for the dervish, for the highest stage of the theologian is to be
sincere in his knowledge and in what he does, for the sake of
God, and to show his sincerity in not seeking any reward for
what he does; he does not experience anything but this. But this
is only the entrance to the Sufi Path. There are many stages and
states that the Sufi must attain until he passes away from his
consideration of all this and from himself, into the contemplation of the Glory of God.

Sha'rani

Ibrahim dreamed he saw the angel Gabriel writing down the
names of the friends of God.

Ibrahim asked, "Is my name there?"

"No," the angel replied.

Ibrahim said, "I am a friend of the friends of God."

Gabriel was silent for a long time. Then he said, "Ibrahim, I
am writing your name at the head of this list."

Attar

At the beginning I was mistaken in four respects. I sought to remember God, to know Him, to love Him, and to seek Him. When
I had come to the end, I saw that He had remembered me before
I remembered Him, that His knowledge of me had preceded my
knowledge of Him, His love toward me had existed before my
love to Him, and He had sought me before I sought Him.

Bayazid Bistami

I thought that I had arrived at the very Throne of God, and I said to it, "O Throne, they tell us that God rests upon thee." "O Bayazid," replied the Throne, "we are told here that He dwells in a humble heart."

Bayazid Bistami

God said, "I loved to be known, so I created creation." This is reflected in the ones whom God loves. The qualities of loving, knowing, hearing, seeing, will, power, talking are all God's gifts to humanity. But God's greatest gift is love, the manifestation of His love of knowing Himself. Love is the primary sustenance for human beings. They cannot live without it, and mankind learned to love from God.

Sheikh Badruddin

A man wished to see the Prophet in a dream, but he could never achieve this vision, no matter how hard he tried. He asked a saint for advice. The saint said, "My son, on Friday evening you must eat a lot of salted fish, then perform your prayer and go to bed without drinking any water. Then you will see."

The man followed this advice. He spent the whole night dreaming that he was drinking from streams, fountains, and springs. When morning came, he ran crying to the saint. "O Master, I did not see the Prophet. I was so thirsty that all I dreamed about was drinking from fountains and springs. I am still on fire with thirst." The saint told him, "So, eating salted fish gave you such a thirst that you dreamed all night long of nothing but water. Now you must feel such a thirst for God's Prophet, and you will then behold his blessed beauty!"

Sheikh Muzaffer

One holiday, the Caliph Harun al-Rashid donned his best robes, mounted his horse, and rode into the streets. The people gave him an ovation, gazing admiringly at his beautifully embroidered robes. At that moment, Bahlul the Wise Fool barred the caliph's progress, reciting the following:

The Festival is not a matter of dressing up in fine new
        clothes,
The Festival is celebrated by serving God and being aware of
        your Lord.
To celebrate the Festival is to be Sultan of the heart, not
        Sultan of the realm.
Sultans of the realm pass into oblivion, but the Sultan of the
        heart is never forgotten.
This brought Harun al-Rashid to tears.

Sheikh Muzaffer

Mary was chosen to bear Jesus because she kept her purity intact. Simple people call this her "virginity," but those who know understand that to be pure means to be completely adaptable, to flow with each moment, to be like a running stream cascading from the waters of life itself. The eternal messenger is always within, waiting to unfold the moment through the Word, and one day when Mary is recognized again, there will be a reappearance of the Christ, manifested in the outer world. Remember who Mary is.

Reshad Feild

Help is always given to the human being; we are always surrounded by the Help of God. The question is to realize it; when it is not known, it is not much use.

Irina Tweedie

CHAPTER 17

Prayer

Prayer is an integral part of all the world's religions. Prayer takes many forms. There are inner and outer forms of prayer. There are silent prayers and prayers that are spoken, chanted, or sung aloud. There are fixed, formal prayers, and spontaneous prayers, inspired by the heart. Behind all real prayer is the sincere heart, longing for God, longing for connection to the Divine.

It is said that everything in the universe is in prayer. All of creation is worshiping God. Only humanity, because we have free will, has the option of praying or not. So, for us, real prayer does not come automatically; it is an achievement.

Keeping our minds focused in prayer is a constant challenge. Unless the heart is on fire, the mind wanders. One day, the Prophet said to his companions, "Can any of you perform even the shortest form of formal prayer and keep your mind solely on God?" (This prayer consists of two sets, each consisting of recitation, followed by bowing once and prostrating twice.) At first no one answered. Finally, the most spiritually advanced of the companions said that he would be willing to try. The Prophet said, "If you can do it, I will *give you my cloak." (The cloak of a prophet is not merely a piece of cloth; it is a sign of spiritual status and even of worthiness to be the prophet's successor.)*

The companion began to pray. At first the Prophet watched him intently. During the second half of the prayer, the Prophet smiled slightly and relaxed. When the man had finished, the Prophet asked him if he was able to keep his mind solely on God. The man replied, "I was able to concentrate on God during the first half of the prayer. But, during the second half, the thought suddenly came to me—the Prophet has two cloaks; which one will I get?"

Some people believe that to miss one of the five daily formal prayers is a sin that will be punished in the Hereafter. The Sufis believe that prayer is an invitation from God, an invitation to the divine presence. Therefore the missing of the prayer is its own punishment. It is like missing a banquet, in this case a banquet for the soul.

⤺

During prayer, God lifts the veils and opens the gates of the invisible, so that His servant is standing in front of Him. The prayer creates a secret connection between the one praying and the One prayed to.

Prayer is a threshold at the entrance to God's reality.

Muhammad

Pray as much as suits your capacity and ability. Do not go to such an extreme that you become ill. The best deed to God is a continuous action, even if it be but a small one.

Muhammad

The following prayer was taught by the Prophet to his companions: "O God, grant me love of You, and to love those who love You, and to love whatever brings me nearer to You. O God, make Your love more precious to me than cool water to the thirsty."

al-Ghazzali

One December in Konya, Rumi had gone into his meditation cell to perform his nighttime prayers. When the time for the morning prayer arrived, he did not appear. His followers became worried because, in twenty years, Rumi had never failed to join them in morning prayer. As time passed and the disciples' alarm grew, someone finally decided to force the door open. Inside, they were startled to find Rum with his beard frozen to the ground, struggling to set himself free. In his prayers, he had begun weeping so copiously that a pool of tears had formed, and his prostration in the cold was so prolonged that the tears froze, trapping him by his beard!

Moinuddin

Once, one of Jesus' apostles was preaching in a small town. The people asked him to perform a miracle, by raising the dead, as Jesus had done.

They went to the town cemetery and stopped before a grave. The apostle prayed to God to bring the dead back to life. The dead man rose from his grave, looked around him, and cried, "My donkey, where is my donkey?" In life, he had been a poor man whose most cherished possession was his donkey.

The same is true for you. Whatever you care about most will determine what happens to you at resurrection. You will be together in the Hereafter with the ones you love.

Sheikh Muzaffer

The high road to God for your spirit, by which your prayers can reach God, is the polishing of the mirror of the heart. The mirror will not become purified from the rust of infidelity and hypocrisy by rebellion and opposition. The mirror is polished by your unwavering faith and your perfect sincerity. Do not confuse the Image with the mirror; they are not the same. The mirror reflects the Image by means of the light, and the light cannot be separated from the Sun, and if the light is not reflected, the fault lies in the mirror.

Whoever remains veiled is like the owl and the sun. If the owl cannot see in the sunlight, it is because of the weakness of its eyes, not because of the sun. He speaks foolishly who does not know that God is manifest in humanity. If you want the mirror to reflect your face, you must hold it straight and keep it bright. Whatever increases the brightness of your heart brings nearer God's manifestation of Himself to you.

Sana'i

Perhaps the Prophet was alluding to this when he said, "One prayer *without you* is better than seventy." That is, a prayer offered without your you-ness excels seventy ordinary ones; for while you remain with yourself, all seventy thousand veils hang before you. But when you are absent from yourself, who remains to be veiled?

'Iraqi

Oh, the one who has fallen in love with gold
Is yelling and screaming,
As if death won't come
And knock at his door.

Think about the day
You are breathing your last breath
And your wife's mind
Is on another husband.
Before the arrow of death pierces your shield,
Make your aim the commandments.
Surrender yourself.

The purpose of humanity
Is observation and understanding.

Oh, God's compassion is raining
Observations and understanding.

Rumi

O my God, what irony it is
That we are at the bottom of hell,
and yet are afraid
of immortality.

Rumi

Once in the course of battle, Ali, the son-in-law of the Prophet,
was struck in the leg by an arrow, which penetrated right
through to the bone. His companions tried to wrench it loose,
but found that it was stuck fast, too firmly pinioned to pull out.
The only solution was to make an incision in the flesh. His rela-
tives said, "We should wait until he prays, because while praying,
Ali is totally unconscious of the world around him." So while he
prayed, they proceeded at once to pinch the flesh, split the bone,
loosen the arrow, and so draw it out.

When the prayers were finished, Ali said, "It seems my pain
has eased somewhat." They then explained how they had removed the arrow while he was absorbed in prayer.

Ansari

GOD'S WOUNDS
Through the great pain of stretching
beyond all that pain has taught me,
the soft well at the base
has opened, and life
touching me there
has turned me into a flower
that prays for rain. Now
I understand: to blossom
is to pray, to wilt and shed

is to pray, to turn to mulch
is to pray, to stretch in the dark
is to pray, to break the surface
after great months of ice
is to pray, and to squeeze love
up the stalky center toward the sky
with only dreams of color
is to pray, and finally to unfold
again as if never before
is to be the prayer.

Mark Nepo

If You were to place before me hellfire, with all it contains of torment, I would think lightly of it in comparison with my state
when You are hidden from me. Forgive the people and do not
forgive me. Have mercy upon them and do not have mercy
upon me. I do not intercede with You for myself or beseech You
for what is due to me. Do with me what You will.

Hallaj

CHAPTER 18

Remembrance of God

In Arabic, repetition and remembrance are the same word. It is said that remembrance of God begins with the repetition of God's Names by the tongue. Then, the repetition of the tongue descends and become the remembrance of the heart. Finally, the remembrance of the heart deepens and becomes the remembrance of the soul. At first, you chant the Divine Names, then they chant themselves, then God chants through you.

There are many different Sufi practices of remembrance, including silent remembrance, chanting of Divine Names, and group practices of chanting, movement, and music.

Implicit in the term remembrance is the notion that we are coming back to what we once knew, what we have already learned. The Sufis believe that our souls were in the world of souls for thousands of years. There, bathed in God's presence, our souls experienced the Divine more fully and deeply than we can imagine. In practicing remembrance, we are seeking to recapture a small part of that blessed state.

Health food enthusiasts insist that you are what you eat. It is also true that you are what you think. By the practice of remembrance of God, eventually the process of remembrance takes hold until you are in a constant state of remembrance. Then, self falls away and God remains.

ᔥ

All creation is calling upon God. You cannot hear or see it on the outside, but the essence in everything is continuously remembering and calling upon God.

Sheikh Muzaffer

When the paintings are hidden, you will see the Painter.

O brother, I will tell you the mystery of mysteries. Know, then, that painting and Painter are one! When your faith is made perfect, you will never see yourself, save in Him.

Attar

Junaid had a young dervish he loved very much, and his older dervishes became jealous. They could not understand what the sheikh saw in the young man. One day, Junaid told all his dervishes to buy a chicken in the marketplace and then kill the chicken. However, they had to kill the chicken where no one could see them. They were to return by sundown at the latest.

One by one the dervishes returned to the sheikh, each with a slaughtered chicken under his arm. Finally, when the sun went down, the young dervish returned, with a live chicken still squawking and struggling. The older dervishes all laughed and whispered among themselves that the young man couldn't even carry out his sheikh's orders!

Junaid asked each of the dervishes to describe how they carried out his instructions. The first man back said that he had gone out and purchased the chicken, then returned home, locked the door, closed the curtains over all the windows, and then killed the chicken. The second dervish said that he returned home with his chicken, locked his door and pulled the curtains, and then he took the chicken into a dark closet and slaughtered it there. The third dervish also took his chicken into the closet, but he blindfolded himself, so he himself could not see the slaughtering. Another dervish went into a dark, deserted area of the forest to sacrifice his chicken. Another went into a pitch black cave.

Finally, it was the young man's turn. He hung his head, embarrassed that he could not follow his sheikh's instructions. "I brought the chicken into my house, but everywhere in the house there was a Presence. I went into the most deserted parts of the forest, but the Presence was still with me. Even in the darkest caves, the Presence was still there. There was no place I could go where I was not seen."

Sheikh Muzaffer

The sheikh of the Halveti order in Istanbul, Sunbul Efendi, in looking for a successor, sent his disciples forth to get flowers to adorn the lodge. All of them returned with large bunches of lovely flowers; only one of them came back with a small, withered plant. When asked why he did not bring anything worthy of his master, he answered, "I found all the flowers busy recollecting the Lord—how could I interrupt this constant prayer of theirs? I looked, and one flower had finished its recollection. That one I brought." It was he who became the next sheikh.

Annemarie Schimmel

I have seen nothing more conducive to righteousness than solitude. He who is alone sees nothing but God, and if he sees nothing but God, nothing moves him but the will of God.

Dhu-l-Nun

One day I was sitting on the edge of a roof when I happened to overhear a woman on another rooftop talking to her husband. She was saying, "It's been some fifty years now that we've dwelled in one house. Whether we had or hadn't, in the heat or in the cold, I was patient, never seeking more than what was right. I never complained to anyone about you. Yet I cannot forgive you this one thing, that you preferred someone else to me. I've done all this for you, that you see *me,* not that you look at somebody else. Today you regarded someone else."

I looked in the Koran to find an analogy for her words and came across the following verse: "We will forgive all your sins, but if in your mind you even faintly incline toward another and put another god beside Me, We will never forgive you."

Hasan al-Basri

If you wish to draw near to God, you must seek God in the hearts of others. You should speak well of all, whether present or absent. If you seek to be a light to guide others, then, like the sun, you must show the same face to all. To bring joy to a single heart is better than to build many shrines for worship, and to enslave one soul by kindness is worth more than the setting free of a thousand slaves.

The true man of God sits in the midst of his fellowmen, and rises up and eats and sleeps and buys and sells and gives and takes in the bazaars, and marries and has social intercourse with others, and yet is never for one moment forgetful of God.

Abu Sa'id

It is easy to know God. But to find the way to God is painfully hard. You cannot find God without passing beyond your own being. A Sufi does not become a Sufi by sitting on a prayer mat. The dervish way is not just the donning of a special turban and cloak. A Sufi is one who annihilates himself in the Truth, one whose heart is purified. The Sufi is someone who needs neither the sun by day nor the moon by night. For the Sufi is one who walks night and day by the Light of Truth. Sufism is poverty that can dispense with property.

How is one to know one's degree of saintliness and vigilance? Only if all parts of one's body join in the Remembrance of God can one be aware of such things. This is the kind of person who is called a Sufi.

Sheikh Muzaffer

I laugh when I hear that the fish in the water is thirsty.

Kabir

The breath that does not repeat the name of God is a wasted breath.

Kabir

Moses asked God to show him one of God's friends. He was told to go to a certain valley. Moses went and found a man dressed in rags, starving, and lice-ridden.

Moses said, "Can I do anything for you?"

The man answered, "Messenger of God, please bring me a cup of water."

When Moses returned with the water, the man had died. He left to look for a piece of cloth to bury him in, and when he returned, Moses found that the body had been mostly devoured by a lion.

Distressed, Moses cried out, "O God, you have made human beings from clay. Some experience great happiness; others are tortured and miserable. No one can understand this paradox."

An inner voice spoke to Moses: "This man relied upon me for everything. Then, he relied on you for drink. He should not have asked for help from another after having been content with me."

Ilahi-Nami

Dhu-l-Nun said to a disciple, "Start instructing people by lecturing, but always remember never to bring yourself [your ego] in between."

The disciple agreed to follow his advice. However, very few attended his discourses. One day nobody came to listen, and he did not deliver a talk that day. Shortly after, an old lady appeared on the spot and, reprimanding him, said, "You had promised to Dhu-l-Nun to deliver a discourse every day and never bring yourself in between. What does your silence mean now? Is this not breaking your solemn promise to him?"

At once he realized his mistake, and thereafter he delivered talks daily for fifty years, never caring whether anyone was present or not.

Attar

There is one thing in this world that must never be forgotten. If you were to forget everything else, but did not forget that, then there would be no cause to worry; whereas if you performed and remembered and did not forget anything else, but forgot that one thing, then you would have done nothing whatsoever.

It is just as if a king had sent you to another country to carry out a specified task. You go and perform a hundred other tasks, but if you have not performed that particular task, it is as though you have done nothing at all.

You have come into this world for a particular task, and that is your purpose; if you do not perform it, then you will have done nothing.

Rumi

You are more precious than both heaven and earth;
You know not your own worth.

Sell not yourself at little price,
Being so precious in God's eyes.

Rumi

Junaid was approached by someone who said, "Be present with me for a while so that I might have a word with you."

Junaid answered, "You want something of me that I have been seeking for some time now. For years, I have wanted to be present for a moment with God, but could not. How then can I be present with you right now?"

Junaid

God says, "I have created you, your moments, your breaths, your possessions, your lives. If they are expended on Me, if you give them to Me, the price of them is everlasting Paradise. This is your worth in My sight."

Rumi

Service

Service is a form of worship—and also a powerful method of self-transformation. Most service that we offer is selfish; it is service for the sake of reward: money, praise, or fame. By service, the Sufis mean service "for God's sake," without any thought of reward. This kind of service comes when we remember that we are a part of God's creation, and that by serving creation we are serving our Creator—not for a heavenly reward, but out of love and gratitude. An old sheikh once said, "Service without love is like a beautiful corpse. The outer form is lovely, but it is lifeless."

Service does not have to be great or dramatic. Years ago, the mother of one of the Ottoman sultans was devoted to charity. She built mosques and a great hospital and had public wells dug in parts of Istanbul that were without water. One day, she went to watch the construction of the hospital she was having built, and she saw an ant fall into the wet concrete of the foundation. She lifted the ant out of the concrete and set it on the ground.

Some years later she passed away. That night she appeared to a number of her friends in their dreams. She was radiant with joy *and inner beauty. Her friends asked her if she had gone to Paradise because of all her wonderful charities, and she replied, "I am in Paradise, but it is not because of those charities. It is for the sake of an ant."*

〜

In the city of Samarkqand there once lived a water carrier who had made a vow: what he earned every Friday, he would give to the poor, for the sake of the souls of his mother and father. Furthermore, he would pray for their forgiveness after each of the five daily prayers. For a long time he honored this commitment, but one Friday he earned no money, so he could give nothing to the poor.

He went and asked a wise man what he ought to do. The man said, "My son, gather up the skins of melons and watermelons. Give them to the animals, then offer the spiritual reward for your actions to your mother and father. That promise of yours will thus be fulfilled."

The water carrier did as the wise man had told him. That very night he saw his mother and father in a dream. "God be pleased with you!" they cried. "You used to send us a present every Friday, and now this Friday night, we received as a divine gift the melons and watermelons of Paradise."

Sheikh Muzaffer

Many sheikhs observe the following rule. When a novice joins them, they subject him to spiritual discipline for three years. He can be admitted to the Path only if he fulfills all the requirements of this discipline. The first year is devoted to service of the people, the second year to service of God, and the third year to watching over his own heart.

Hujwiri

One evening a sheikh was talking about humility and service. He spoke eloquently about service and putting others' needs before our own. Then, someone asked, "What do you do with the arrogant? How can you serve the arrogant?"

The sheikh drew himself up and raised his powerful voice, "With the arrogant, you must behave arrogantly!" Everyone was shocked.

Then, the sheikh went on, "To treat the arrogant with humility would be like giving them poison. It would only feed their arrogance."

Sheikh Muzaffer

In prebiblical times, a young man once got married. The Prophet of that people, who performed the wedding, told his companions that this young man was to die that very night. Next morning, the bridegroom came to worship, to the astonishment of those present. The Prophet asked the young man whether he had put away his mattress and bedding. "No," the man replied.

The Prophet then took his companions to the young man's house. He turned over the bedding, and there was a poisonous snake lying under the mattress. The Prophet addressed the snake, "What are you doing here? Why did you come here?" Everyone heard the snake answer, "I was sent to bite this young man, but I was bound with an iron chain. Try as I might, I could not escape from the chain."

The Prophet turned to the young bridegroom and asked, "What good have you done recently?" The man replied, "I gave a cup of milk to a beggar who came to my door last night." The Prophet said, "You see, that act of charity saved you!"

Sheikh Muzaffer

Someone asked the Prophet, "Who has the greater right over children, the mother or the father?" He answered, "The mother's right is greater than the father's." He was asked three times, and each time the answer was the same. The fourth time, he said, "The father's right is next."

"Why do you give the mother three rights to the father's one?"

The Prophet replied, "Your mother carried you for nine months in her womb, then gave you birth. After that she gave up her sleep for you, suckled you, carried you in her arms, and cleaned you. For years she cooked for you, fed you, and served you food. She did your laundry. When you were forty, fifty, sixty, she still followed your progress with interest. Your father sowed you in your mother's womb, provided your food, and made sure you had clothes to wear. Can this be compared with your mother's role?"

The questioner went on, "Well, I wonder if I could ever repay my mother for all the help and service, however much I might do for her?" The Prophet replied, "You could not repay so much as one night's due!"

"But suppose I carry my mother on my back for years, clean up after her, cook for her, and feed her. Suppose I attend to those same services as long as she may live?"

"There will still be this difference between you: your mother looked out for you to live, while you are waiting for her to die."

Sheikh Muzaffer

The first duty is to behave with purity of intention. It should never be forgotten that every deed and every action is judged according to the intention behind it. Therefore, whatever the lover does, whatever action the lover performs, must be done for the sake of God. Actions performed with complete sincerity and for God's sake are accepted and approved. But deeds that are done to be seen by others and to win their praise and love may be adulterated with hypocrisy.

Sheikh Muzaffer

The Children of Israel once said to Moses, "O Moses, we want to invite our Lord to a meal. Speak to God so that He may accept our invitation!" Moses angrily replied, "Don't you know that God is beyond the need for food?" But when Moses ascended Mount Sinai, God said to him, "Why did you not inform me of the invitation? My servants have invited me; tell them I shall come to their feast on Friday evening."

Moses told the people, and everyone began making great preparations for days. On Friday evening, an old man arrived, weary from a long journey. "I am so hungry," he said to Moses. "Please give me something to eat." Moses said, "Be patient. The Lord of all Worlds is coming. Take this jug and fetch some water. You can also help serve." The old man brought water and again asked for food, but no one would feed him before the Lord arrived. It got later and later, and finally, everyone began criticizing Moses for misleading them.

Moses climbed Mount Sinai and said, "My Lord, I have been put to shame before everyone because You did not come as You promised You would." God replied, "I did come. I actually approached you yourself, but when I told you I was hungry, you sent Me to fetch water. I asked again but was sent away to serve. Neither you nor your people were able to welcome Me with honor."

"My Lord, an old man came and asked me for food. But he was a mere mortal."

"I was together with that servant of Mine. To have honored him would have been to honor Me. To have served him would have been to serve Me. All the heavens are too small to contain Me, but not the hearts of My servants. I neither eat nor drink, yet to honor my servant is to honor Me. To care for them is to care for Me."

Sheikh Muzaffer

Serving God—what more beautiful thing is there to do! The only real joy is to be a servant of God, and that means being awake all the time to the needs of the moment. If we are asleep, then we will never know what is required of us. We cannot have any preconceived ideas of what service means. We never know from one moment to the next what will be asked of us. When you enter the path you put yourself in the street of service for the rest of your life. There is no going back. Do not think that you can be of service only when you want to be of service! You must be awake to the needs of the moment, God's needs, not to your own needs. Only then may you be granted the privilege of being of service.

Sheikh Muzaffer

I once had a brother in Iraq. I would go to him when times were bad and say, "Give me some of your money." He would throw me his purse for me to take what I wanted. Then one day I came to him and said, "I need something." He asked, "How much do you want?" And so the sweetness of brotherhood left my heart.

al-Ghazzali

There was once a man whose father was an aged invalid. The man's wife was forever demanding, "Your father is too much trouble. I can't take care of him all the time. Either he goes or I go!" The poor husband would implore, "What can I do? If I don't look after him, who will?"

The woman insisted that unless he took action she would leave him the next day. Reluctantly, the man decided to abandon his father in the mountains. He got his cart ready and said to his father, "I am going to take a trip to the mountains with my son. Why don't you come with us?"

The three set off together. The old man chatted with his grandson, and the two had a great time together. When they reached the mountains, the man spread bedding on the ground for his father and set a little food and water beside him. "Just lie there, father, while we go and chop firewood."

Then, the man took his son and headed back toward home. "Why did we leave Grandfather all alone?" asked the boy. "Aren't we going back to fetch him?" The man replied, "He has grown old. We are going to let him stay there." "But why?" cried the child. "I want my grandfather!"

His father insisted, "He is too old, I tell you! He has to stay there. . . ." The child replied thoughtfully, "Very well, when I grow up, you will be old and sickly like Grandfather. When that time comes, shall I leave you in the mountains like you left Grandfather?"

Realizing now what he had done, the man went back, weeping. He fell at his father's feet. The old man caressed his son's head, saying, "Don't cry, my son. I did not leave *my* father in the mountains, so why should God make you leave *me* here?"

Sheikh Muzaffer

PART 7

Faces of the One

CHAPTER 20

God

What is not God?

Look around in every direction. Look at the people you know: the shining beings, the simple souls, the sad, the angry, the gentle, the kind, the cruel. Look at the smallest creatures: fleas, dust mites, viruses, bacteria. Look inside yourself: at your thoughts, feelings, memories, opinions, reflections, and dreams. What is not God?

Whatever you answer, whatever you identify as "not God"— Hitler, breast cancer, garbage dumped on your lawn, your father-in-law's temper, your own indolence—by separating these from what you think is God, you are missing the essential point. Everything is infused with God. Everything is animated by God. Everything is a facet, a reflection, of the Divine.

There are no idols or images in Islam. Whatever you see, within or without, is a manifestation of God. The Sufi lives in a world of true monotheism. This homage to a single deity is not to be compared with the theoretical monotheism of Christianity, with the holy Trinity, the plethora of saints, and the nine ranks of angels.

At the center of Sufi prayer, of service, and of daily life, one truth resounds—there is nothing, created or uncreated, that is not God.

⇔

If you walk toward Him, He comes to you running.

Muhammad

Wheresoever you turn, there is the face of Allah.

Koran

I don't know what sort of a God we have been talking about.
The caller calls in a loud voice to the Holy One at dusk.
Why? Surely the Holy One is not deaf.
He hears the delicate anklets that ring on the feet of an insect
        as it walks.
Go over and over your beads, paint weird designs on your
        forehead,
wear your hair matted, long, and ostentatious,
but when deep inside you there is a loaded gun, how can you
        have God?

Kabir

Rose and mirror and sun and moon—where are they?
Wherever we looked, there was always Thy face.

Mir

I am the companion of him who remembers Me.

Muhammad

Those who adore God in the sun behold the sun, and those
who adore Him in living things see a living thing, and those
who adore Him in lifeless things see a lifeless thing, and those
who adore Him as a Being unique and unparalleled see that which has

no like. Do not attach yourself to a particular creed exclusively so that you disbelieve in all the rest; otherwise you will lose much good; nay, you will fail to recognize the real truth of the matter. God, the omnipresent and omnipotent, is not limited by any one creed. Wheresoever you turn, there is the face of Allah.

Ibn 'Arabi

The eyes that regard God are also the eyes through which He regards the world.

Traditional

When a servant whom God loves prays to Him, God says, "O Gabriel, delay answering the need of My servant, for I love to hear his voice."

When a servant whom God dislikes prays to Him, God says, "O Gabriel, answer my servant's needs, for I dislike hearing his voice."

Traditional

"O my Lord, if I worship Thee for fear of hell, burn me in hell; and if I worship Thee for hope of Paradise, exclude me thence; but if I worship Thee for Thine own sake, withhold not from me Thine eternal Beauty."

Rabia

A dervish had been walking for weeks and finally came to the foot of a mountain. He raised his hands and prayed, "Oh Lord, please send me a donkey to help me up this hill."

Just then, he heard the sound of braying, and he found a small donkey caught in the bushes. The dervish thanked God for the gift and was just about to get on the donkey when a bandit rode up.

The bandit said, "Aha, a dervish. I never liked dervishes! Here you are, a big man about to ride that little donkey. Better that the donkey should ride you than you should ride the donkey. Yes, that's it! Pick up the donkey and put it on your back."

The dervish looked at the bandit in dismay. "Pick up the donkey?"

The bandit put his hand on his scimitar. "I said pick it up and put it on your back!"

The dervish reluctantly complied; then the bandit growled, "Now, carry the donkey up the mountain."

The dervish walked up the mountain with the donkey on his back. Finally, the poor, exhausted dervish reached the top. He set the donkey down and addressed God. "Lord, I know that You see everything and that You know everything. But sometimes You get it backward!"

Sheikh Muzaffer

A woodcutter was walking with a heavy load on his back. At length he dropped to the ground and, throwing himself wearily down, began to bemoan his fate. "O God," he cried, "either send me a donkey or send me death!" Just at the moment a huge boulder came rolling down the mountainside and landed a few feet from him. "So!" he exclaimed in fear and anger, "You haven't the power to give me a donkey, but you're quite clever enough to kill me!"

Bakatiyari

He heals our nature from within,
kinder to us than we ourselves are.
His kindness makes the worthless worthy;
and in return he is content
with his servants' gratitude and patience.
You have broken faith,
yet still he keeps his faith with you:
he is truer to you
than you are to yourself.

Sana'i

One night, while Hasan was praying, he heard a voice cry, "Ha! Abu 'l-Hasan! Do you wish Me to tell the people what I know about you? They may stone you to death." "O Lord God," he replied, "do You wish me to tell the people what I know of Thy mercy and what I perceive of Thy grace, that none of them need ever again bow to Thee in prayer?" The voice answered, "Keep your secret, and I will keep Mine."

Khurqani

IS SOMETHING MISSING?
Anyone can say anything.
Eyes look without obstruction,
and the nose, it sniffs everything.

Legs go where they want to. Hands reach.
The mind respects nothing. Even the heart
is unsure where to stand. This is how
things are. Is something missing?

A human being can walk in different ways.
Deliberately, as though going somewhere,
or strolling with no purpose, or marching,
or limping, or pretending to be a gorilla
with arms hanging down.

He or she can curse you or trust you, comfort you,
or act without considering anything or anyone.
Truth and lies, both glitter in the eyes.
He or she can hear and enjoy and embrace
the language coming in, but to understand everything
with divine wisdom is hard.

There is one clear truth, the pure loving.
When people do not have that, they are
disconnected. Words are just words,
and good actions are done for wrong reasons.

Paint on a red dot like the dancing Shiva,
but if you don't know how to open your heart
with modesty, dignity, and respect for others,
it's just collecting more honors and robes.

It's easy to explain the condition of being human,
what's missing and what's here, but if
you don't know God exists,
it's foolishness.

To know this and act accordingly is difficult.
Saying the words is easy.

Bawa Muhaiyaddeen

'Umar 'Abu'l-Aziz once wrote a letter to Hasan al-Basri in which
he requested some brief advice that would serve to guide him.
On the back of the envelope, Hasan wrote, "O Commander of
the Faithful, if God is with you, then what do you fear, and if
God isn't with you, in what can you have hope?"

Hasan al-Basri

The Sufi becomes more humble every hour, for every hour is
drawing him nearer to God. The Sufis see without knowledge,
without sight, without information received, and without observation, without description, without veiling and without veil.
They are not themselves, but insofar as they exist at all, they
exist in God. Their movements are caused by God, and their
words are the words of God uttered by their tongues, and their
sight is the sight of God, which has entered into their eyes. So
God Most High has said, "When I love a servant, I, the Lord, am
his ear so that he hears by Me, I am his eye so that he sees by
Me, and I am his tongue so that he speaks by Me, and I am his
hand so that he takes by Me."

Dhu-l-Nun

Tear aside veils of all you see in this world, and you will find yourself apart in solitude with God. If you draw aside the veils of the stars and the spheres, you will see that all is one with the Essence of your own pure soul. If you will but tear aside the veil, you will see nonexistence, and you will see forthwith the true meaning of God's purpose. When you have cast aside the veil, you will see the Essence, and all things will be shown forth within the Essence. If you draw aside the veil from the Face of the Beloved, all that is hidden will be made manifest, and you will become one with God, for then will you be the very Essence of the Divine.

Attar

Allah's essence in its uniqueness is free from any resemblance to anything else. It is by Itself and known only to Itself. It cannot even be described as all and everything, or as the one and only thing. But Allah's attributes are manifested as the reality in all and everything in the universe, and the whole is within the smallest element in the making of the whole.

All the energy and power within everything is locked in its smallest particle; in every atom the divine power is hidden. Yet the whole is not visible, for the fire is hidden within the flint, and within the seed is the entire tree.

Sheikh Badruddin

Whoever finds it astonishing
that God should save him from his passion
or yank him out of his forgetfulness
has deemed the divine Power to be weak.

Ibn Ata 'Illah

Before this there was one heart
  but a thousand thoughts.
Now all is reduced to:
  There is no god but God.

       Iraqi

CHAPTER 21

Satan

In Islam, Satan is identified as the single angel who, setting himself apart from all other angelic beings, refused God's command to bow down before Adam on the day of his creation. When questioned by the Creator as to why he disobeyed, the Devil answered that he bowed down solely to the Divine, not to any of the created. Unrepentant, he also argued that God's will determines all things, so it would not have been possible for him to refuse God's command unless God himself had allowed him to do so.

For this, he was banished from Heaven and was taken away from the presence of God. No more does the eye of God enlighten him; no more will the touch of God give him joy.

But in spite of this punishment, he has never lost his love for God.

He alone, of all the beings in the cosmos, loves God without gain, without hope, without even the possibility of feeling loved in return. Thus, seen objectively, this unrequited love is the most pure of any. The Devil serves without reward.

Even while bearing the burden of eternal separation, the Devil has taken on the thankless and usually misunderstood task of creating obstacles for human beings. What few realize is that, through rising above these obstacles, we are able to rise to where he cannot go, stepping over him in our ascent toward our own higher natures. The Devil toughens us, forces us to remain awake, and offers lessons as no other angel can. Would we ever have learned to walk if our parents had continued to carry us everywhere? Our troubles and temptations, even if truly given to us by the Devil, are still ultimately gifts of God.

⮑

Rabia was asked, "Do you love the Lord of Glory?"

She said, "I do."

Then she was asked, "Do you hold Satan as an enemy?"

She replied, "No."

The questioner was astonished. "How is that?"

Rabia said, "My love of God leaves not room for hating Satan." She went on: "I saw the Prophet in a dream, and he said to me, 'O Rabia, do you love me?' I said, 'O Prophet of God, who is there who does not love thee? But my love to God has so possessed me that no place remains for loving or hating any save Him.'"

Attar

Someone asked Satan, "O wretched one, when it became apparent that you had been cursed, why did you accept it so wholeheartedly in your heart like a treasure?" Satan replied, "A curse is the King's arrow. When he fires it he looks to the target. If you have eyes, look at the archer's target, not at his arrow."

Attar

Satan said, "Everything depends upon God's favor and discretion, not on the effort and devotion of the devotee. I was commanded to prostrate before Adam, and I did not do so; Adam was ordered not to eat from that tree, yet he did so. Favor was at work in Adam's case; God forgave him, saying, 'We made a covenant with Adam in ancient times, but he forgot.' Whereas in my case, favor was withheld, and God said, 'He refused and was proud.' Adam's error was not counted, while my sustained devotion had no weight in the balance at all."

Khanass

"O Satan," said Moses, "do you love God?"

He replied, "Every time his love increases toward someone else, my love and devotion increases toward him."

"O Satan," said Moses, "do you remember him?"

He answered, "I am the one remembered by him, to whom he said, 'My curse be upon you!' Do not the 'you' and the 'I' coexist in that curse? I am pledged to loving and yearning. I am in heaven and hell."

"O Satan," said Moses, "how is it that despite your cursed existence, your words are sweet?"

"My experiences," replied Satan, "are those of one who has been tested, Moses. I worshiped God for seven hundred thousand years, craving a better position with him. My craving in devotion brought about my destruction. I stopped craving, and now my remembrance is keener, my devotion sweeter. O Moses, do you know why God has caused me to be separated? So that I would not mix with the sincere ones and worship him out of passion or fear or hope or craving."

Sana'i

Abdul Qadir al-Jilani one morning was still asleep at the time for the morning prayer. A cat came over to his side and nudged

him until he awoke. Noticing the lateness of the time, Abdul
Qadir quickly made his prayers. When he had finished, he
looked at the cat. With his spiritual insight, he saw that the cat
was actually a devil. This puzzled the great saint. So he asked, "I
can see you are a devil, but why on earth did you wake me for
the prayer?"

The cat answered, "Because you've discovered me, I might as
well tell you. I knew that if you missed your obligatory prayer,
you would offer one hundred prayers as compensation, so I
woke you up so that you would get only the benefits of the one."

Abdul Qadir al-Jilani

The Devil keeps hammering his subtle persuasions until the
learned man becomes convinced that he should set about teaching people. Then the Devil intimates to the scholar, "You should
embellish your thoughts with pretty language and impressive
conceits. Also play up your qualifications. Otherwise your words
won't have much effect; they won't reach people's hearts and
they will not succeed in attaining the truth."

al-Ghazzali

Satan said, "Because this keepsake was given to me by my
Beloved, I don't care if it is good or bad. Anyone who distin-
guishes between the two is still immature in love. From the hand
of the Friend it matters not whether it is honey or poison, sweet
or sour, grace or wrath. When the King bestows his own special
cloak and cap on the lover, nothing else matters."

Hallaj

A pious woodcutter once heard about a tribe of nearby pagans
who worshiped a tree. He decided to cut it down. As the woodcutter was on his way to cut down the tree, the Devil came up to
him and asked, "Where are you going?"

The woodcutter said, "I am going to cut that tree down."

The Devil said, "No, no, don't do it."

"Who are you to tell me what to do? I am going to chop down that tree for God's sake."

The Devil said, "I am the Devil. I told you not to do that. I am not going to let you cut down that tree."

The woodcutter cried, "You! You cannot stop me." He grabbed the Devil and threw him to the ground. The man sat on the Devil's chest and put his ax on the Devil's throat, fully prepared to kill him.

The Devil said, "You are very unreasonable. You are going to try to chop down that tree, but the tribe will not let you cut down their god. They may even kill you. Then your family will be left destitute. Be reasonable. Leave this project of yours. I'll make a bargain with you. I know that you make only two coppers a day as a woodcutter. You are a devout man and you have a big family, and also you like to help people. Every morning I will put under your bed two gold coins. Instead of going and getting yourself killed, you can spend the money on your family's needs and also help the poor.

The woodcutter replied, "I don't believe you. You are going to cheat me. Everybody knows the Devil is a cheat and a liar. You just want to save yourself."

The Devil said, "No I am not going to cheat you. Besides, try me. If you don't find two gold coins each morning, you can always take your ax and chop down the tree."

The man agreed. The next morning, he found two brand-new gold coins under his mattress. He bought food and clothing for his family and distributed the remainder to the poor. The next morning, when he looked under the mattress, he found nothing. He searched all over the bedroom, but found no gold coins.

Angrily, the woodcutter took up his ax and set off to chop down the tree. On the road, he met the Devil again. The Devil asked, "Where do you think you are going?"

"You cheat, you liar! I am going to chop down that tree!"

The Devil tapped the man on the chest with his finger, and the woodcutter was knocked over. The Devil said, "Do you want me to kill you now? I want you to promise not to harm that tree."

"Oh no, don't kill me. I won't touch the tree. But I just want to ask you one thing. Two days ago I defeated you easily. I just grabbed you and threw you down. Where did you get this tremendous force today?"

"Listen carefully. The other day, you were going to cut that tree for God's sake. Today you were fighting me for the sake of two gold coins."

Sheikh Muzaffer

PART 8

Transformation

CHAPTER 22

Self-Transformation

The goal of self-transformation is to remove all the veils between us and God. The final veil is the "I," the sense of separateness we each carry. To remove this is far from easy. Ask yourself, "How can I take 'I' out of me?"

The great Sufi philosophers insist that our sense of individuality is an illusion, that there is only one Reality, which is God. So self-transformation is to remove all illusions, including the final illusion, self, in order to experience Reality. Those who see Sufism as a path of love say the same thing in other words. For them, the goal is for the beloved, lover, and love to become one.

Most of us believe that we are basically all right as we are. We just need a little more money, a little more love, a little more free time—then we will be just fine. The Sufis believe that this is far from the truth. We all need fundamental change; we need to hatch into a whole new level of being. Unless we recognize the deep, transformational nature of the work we need to do, we are fated to waste all our efforts. We have developed the psychology of the chicken when what we really need is the psychology of the egg.

The metamorphosis of caterpillar into butterfly is a particularly good metaphor for self-transformation. At a certain point the caterpillar feels impelled to wrap itself in a cocoon. Immobile, it begins to dissolve. There is no sense of a marvelous new life that is coming; there is only the dissolving of the old, and the deep fears that accompany this. The caterpillar literally turns into a kind of goo, and only from that annihilation of the old form can the magnificent new form of the butterfly emerge.

We can get a sense of this radical process of self-transformation from those who have been through it, and be guided by those who can help us through this process.

⇔

If you could get rid
Of yourself just once,
The secret of secrets
Would open to you.
The face of the unknown,
Hidden beyond the universe
Would appear on the
Mirror of your perception.

Rumi

Realize that you know nothing and you are nobody. It is no easy thing to attain this realization. It doesn't come with teaching and instruction, nor can it be sewn on with a needle, or tied with a thread. This is a gift from God and a question of whom He bestows it on and whom He causes to experience it.

Abu Sa'id

A man asked Rabia, "If I repent, will God accept my repentance?"

Rabia replied at once, "No, but if He turns toward you, you will turn toward Him."

Rabia

Bayazid said, "Paradise is of no worth to those who love." Rabia had a related saying: "First the neighbor, then the house." That is, the neighbor, or God, is more important than the house, or Paradise.

Attar

"The first time I entered the Holy House," said Bayazid, "I saw the Holy House. The second time I entered it, I saw the Lord of the House. The third time I saw neither the House nor the Lord of the House."

By this Bayazid meant, "I became lost in God, so that I knew nothing. Had I seen at all, I would have been God." Proof of this interpretation is given by the following anecdote:

A man came to the door of Bayazid and called out.

"Whom are you seeking?" asked Bayazid.

"Bayazid," replied the man.

"Poor wretch!" said Bayazid. "I have been seeking Bayazid for thirty years, and cannot find any trace or token of him."

Bayazid Bistami

So complete was Bayazid's absorption in God that, every day when he was called by a disciple who had been his inseparable companion for twenty years, he would say, "My son, what is your name?"

"Master," the disciple said one day, "you are mocking me. For twenty years I have been serving you, and every day you ask me my name."

"My son," replied Bayazid, "I do not deride you. But His Name has entered my heart and has expelled all other names. As soon as I learn a new name, I promptly forget it."

Attar

Between me and You there lingers an "it is I"
      which torments me.

Ah! lift through mercy this "it is I"
    from between us both!

Hallaj

The *zhikrs* [repetitions of Divine Names] are becoming even deeper; in the truest sense of the word, they are taking on "substance." This is where the inner peace unfolds, the peace described so beautifully by Islam as the tranquillity of the heart. Right above the heart region is where you feel it, as if pulling open curtains on either side. . . . So is this the "polishing of the heart"?

Sometimes it feels as if I'm penetrating directly into the syllables of the holy formulas, into the sound that echoes silently within me. The greater the awareness, the more intense the experience is. The *zhikr* is showing me how to do *zhikrs!* The old precept comes to mind: "At first you act as if you're doing the *zhikr*. Then you do the *zhikr*. Then finally the *zhikr* does you." All at once I perceive this steering process as one of the "signs" of Allah: *"He is closer to you than your jugular vein."* Where can one perceive Him Who is immanent and transcendent if not in one's deepest insides? The signs of which the Holy Koran speaks are *"on the horizons and within yourselves."* Is that it? "His Heaven and His Earth cannot contain Him," says Islam, "only the heart of the believer has room for Him."

Suddenly it becomes painfully clear to me. There's really only one way: absolute surrender, absolute giving-up of wanting-for-oneself.

Ozelsel

The Sufi is he to whom nothing is attached, and who does not become attached to anything.

Nuri

You ought to know yourself as you really are, so that you may understand of what nature you are, from where you have come to this world, for what purpose you were created, and in what your happiness and misery consist. For within you are combined the qualities of the animals and the wild beasts and also the qualities of the angels, but the spirit is your real essence, and all beside it is, in fact, foreign to you.

Strive for knowledge of your origin, so that you may know how to attain to the Divine Presence and the contemplation of the Divine Majesty and Beauty. Deliver yourself from the fetters of lust and passion. God did not create you to be their captive; they should be your servants, under your control for the journey that is before you, to be your steed and your weapon, so that you may use them to pursue your happiness, and when you have not more need of them, then cast them under your feet.

A Sufi began to weep in the middle of the night. He said, "The world is like a closed casket in which we are placed and in which, through our ignorance, we spend our time in folly. When Death opens the lid of the casket, each one who has wings takes his flight to Eternity, but that one who is without wings remains in the casket. Before the lid is taken away from this casket, become a bird of the Way to God. Develop your wings and your feathers. No, rather burn your wings and your feathers and destroy yourself by fire, and so will you arrive at the Goal before all others."

Attar

The first step is to say, "God," and nothing else; the second is intimacy; and the third is to burn.

Attar

One night, the moths gathered together, tormented by their longing to unite themselves with the candle. They all said, "We must find someone to give us news of that for which we long so earnestly."

One of the moths then went to a castle and saw the light of a candle within. He returned and told the others what he had seen. But the wise moth, the chief of their assembly, said, "He has no real information to give us about the candle." Another moth then visited the candle and passed close to the light, drawing near to it and touching the flame with his wings. He, too, came back and explained something of what union with the candle meant, but the wise moth said to him, "Your explanation is really worth no more than your comrade's."

A third moth rose up, and threw himself violently into the candle's flame. He hurled himself forward and stretched out his antennae toward the fire. As he entered completely into its embrace, his members became glowing red like the flame itself. The wise moth saw from afar that the candle had identified the moth with itself and had given the moth its own light. He said, "This moth alone understands that to which he has attained. None other knows it, and this is all."

In truth, it is the one who has lost all knowledge and trace of his own existence who has, at the same time, found knowledge of the Beloved. So long as you will not ignore your own body and soul, how will you ever know the Object you love?

Attar

It is better to lose your life in the quest than to languish miserably. If we should not succeed, but die of grief, ah well, so much the worse, but, because errors are numerous in this world, we may at least avoid acquiring new ones.

Thousands of creatures are craftily occupied in the pursuit of the dead body of the world; so, if you give yourself up to this commerce, above all with guile, will you be able to make your heart an ocean of love?

Some say that the wish for spiritual things is presumption, and that no mere upstart can attain them. But isn't it better to sacrifice one's life in pursuit of this desire than to be identified with a business?

So long as we do not die to ourselves, and so long as we are identified with someone or something, we shall never be free.

Attar

FREEFALL
If you have one hour of air
and many hours to go,
you must breathe slowly.

If you have one arm's length
and many things to care for,
you must give freely.

If you have one chance to know God
and many doubts, you must
set your heart on fire.

We are blessed.

Each day is a chance.
We have two arms.
Fear wastes air.

Mark Nepo

Passing away [loss of self in the Divine] and *continuance* [remaining in divine communion in the midst of worldly activity] are two terms applicable to the servant who acknowledges that God is One. The first level of meaning of *passing away* and *continuance* is the passing away of ignorance into the abiding condition of knowledge and the passing away of disobedience into the abiding state of obedience and the passing away of indifference into the state of continual worship and the passing away of the consideration of the actions of the servant, which are temporary, into the vision of the divine Grace, which is eternal.

al-Sarraj

At a court banquet, everyone was sitting according to their rank, waiting for the king to appear. A simply dressed man came in and took a seat above everyone else. The prime minister demanded that he identify himself.

"Are you the adviser of a great king?"

"No, I rank above a royal adviser."

"Are you a prime minister?"

"No, I outrank a prime minister."

"Are you a king in disguise?"

"No, I am above that rank as well."

"Then you must be God," the prime minister said sarcastically.

"No, I am above that."

"There is nothing above God!" shouted the prime minister.

The stranger replied calmly, "Now you know me. That *nothing* is me."

Traditional

I came out of Bayazid-ness as a snake from its skin. Then I looked. I saw that lover, Beloved, and love are one because in that state of unification all can be one.

Bayazid Bistami

First He pampered me with a hundred favors,
Then he melted me with the fires of sorrows.
After He sealed me with the seal of Love,
I became Him.
Then, he threw my self out of me.

Rumi

CHAPTER 23

Death

For Sufis, death is not a transition; it is stepping across a threshold and being given another chance to reawaken. Life, as well, offers a spectrum of opportunities, that, if taken, allow one to recover awareness of one's full identity.

Huston Smith calls Sufis the "impatient ones," those who are not willing to wait to be reunited with Divinity at death but hunger for union now. "Why the rush?" the rest of us might inquire. Who looks forward with equanimity to his or her own death?

If you accept the premise that life and death are both gifts, then the prospect of death can become more a source of wonder than a cause for fear.

It is especially hard for Americans to think in this way, because our culture is almost as phobic about death as that of ancient Egypt. Egyptians packed off their dead into tombs full of belongings, mummifying their dead to prevent physical decay. We do much the same, making our dead look as good or better than they did in life, then preserving their flesh in soft, padded containers as long-lasting and as secure as we can afford. In the face of culturally sanctioned denial, how can we possibly see death as a gift?

There is a medieval Christian mystery play in which the lead character asks who will come with him into the grave to support him at his last judgment.

"Not I," said his friends.

"Not I," said his children.

"Not I," said his wife.

"Not I," said his priest.

"Not I," said his fields of grain, his cattle and his sheep, his gold, and all his treasures.

"I will stay with you, " said his Actions, upon which they leapt into the grave to be by his side. Arm in arm, they knocked at the door of death—together.

What do you take with you into the city of death? Not a suitcase, not a purse, not even the pictures in your wallet. You never see a hearse followed by a moving van. Nothing goes with you except the sum of what your life has been.

A Sufi teaching says, "Die before you die." One interpretation is that you should strive to learn what you would be shown at death while you still have time to make use of this knowledge, that is, while still alive in a body. The wisdom we achieve on death reveals the true value of what is important and what is not. How much richer life becomes if we are able to gain this perspective beforehand.

∽

One day a dervish came to Attar's pharmacy. He saw the clutter and display; he smelled the heady scent of herbs and perfumes; then he heaved a deep sigh and began to weep.

Disturbed by such odd sight, Attar asked the dervish to move on.

The dervish replied, "All right, sir. My load is light, nothing more than this old garment I am wearing. But you, Attar, my heart aches for you! When the time comes for you to depart, how are you going to carry all these goods?"

Farzan

When the angel of death came to take Abraham's soul, Abraham said, "Have you ever seen a friend take his friend's life?"

God answered him, "Have you ever seen a friend unwilling to meet or go with his friend?"

al-Ghazzali

PRACTICING

As a man in his last breath
drops all he is carrying

each breath is a little death
that can set us free.

Mark Nepo

The sitting one is a shopkeeper,
the standing one herds cows,
the wakeful one is a watchman!
Death grabbed and ate them all.

Kabir

Death is a bridge whereby the lover rejoins the Beloved.

Rabia

Somebody once came to the venerable companion Abu Darda, saying, "I want to be a good man, but my heart is sick. O imam, prescribe for me a remedy."

Abu Darda said to him, "My son, perform the funeral prayer, go around to hospitals, and visit the cemeteries. This will cure your malady." The man acted on this advice.

If people could be reformed by performing funeral prayer, the funeral imams would be saints. If visiting the tombs would bring people to the Truth, grave diggers would be angels. If visits to the sick made people human, nurses we would be perfect human beings.

The man performed the funeral prayer in the same way as our funeral imams. His visits to the tombs were like those of the grave diggers. He visited the sick like a hospital attendant. And yet his heart stayed dark. Then he went and complained to Abu Darda: "O imam, I followed that advice of yours, but my heart is as hard as ever. I derived no benefit whatever."

To this Abu Darda replied, "As you were performing the funeral prayer, did it occur to you to think, 'It is I who am lying in this coffin; these prayers are for my funeral'? Did you say to yourself, 'It is I they have stripped naked; it is I who have been deprived of wealth and rank; my wife is a widow, my children are orphans; they are putting me away in the dark earth, I have no will of my own; they have bound me without rope or chains; here I am alone with my deeds; now the two angels will come and question me; what am I to do alone in this house of darkness'?"

The man said, "No, I thought of no such thing."

Abu Darda then told him, "You will gain nothing from performing the funeral prayer as you did. On the contrary, it will blacken your heart. Now go and do it again, thinking of these things."

Sheikh Muzaffer

One dies when, by Allah's will, one's borrowed time ends. One's material being—which is called life—ending at an appointed hour, loses all its character and qualities both good and bad, and nothing remains. In their place Allah comes to be. One's self becomes Allah's self; one's attributes become Allah's attributes.

That is what the Prophet of Allah (peace and blessings be upon him) meant when he said, "Die before dying."

Ibn 'Arabi

Remember your contemporaries who have passed away and were of your age.

Remember the honors and fame they earned, the high posts they held, and the beautiful bodies they possessed. Today all of them are turned to dust. They have left orphans and widows behind them, their wealth is being wasted, and their houses turned into ruins.

No sign of them is left today, and they lie in the dark holes underneath the earth.

Picture their faces before your mind's eye and ponder.

Do not fix hopes on your health, and do not laugh away life. Remember how they walked and now all their joints lie separated and the tongue with which they talked lightly is eaten away by the worms.

al-Ghazzali

A man was sitting beside the venerable Solomon when Azra-il came and gave him a look that filled him with fear and dread. When Solomon told him it was the Angel of Death, the man said, "O Prophet of Allah, I am very much afraid of him. Send me away to China so that I can be as far away from him as possible."

The venerable Solomon commanded the wind to carry that man away to China. A little later, Azra-il came back, and Solomon asked him, "Why did you give that man such a look when you came here a while ago?"

The Angel of Death replied, "I was under orders to take that man's soul from him in China, so I was surprised to see him sitting beside you in Jerusalem."

Sheikh Muzaffer

When someone brought information to Nushirvan the Just that an enemy of his had been removed from this world by God the Most High, he asked, "Have you heard anything about his intending to spare me?"

Nushirvan

When you see my funeral, don't say, "What a separation!"
It is time for me to visit and meet the Beloved.
Since you have seen my descent, then do see my rising.
Why complain about the setting of the moon and the sun?
Which seed that went under the earth failed to grow up again?

Rumi

For my funeral:
Call the drummers, timbal beaters, and tambourine players.
March toward my grave dancing thus,
Happy, gay, intoxicated; with hands clapping,
So that people would know that the friends of God
Go happy and smiling toward the place of meeting.

Rumi

Friend, hope for the Guest while you are alive.
Jump into experience while you are alive!
Think . . . and think . . . while you are alive.
What you call "salvation" belongs to the time before death.
If you don't break your ropes while you are alive,
do you think
ghosts will do it after?
The idea that the soul will join with the ecstatic
just because the body is rotten—
that is all fantasy.
What is found now is found then.
If you find nothing now,
you will simply end up with an apartment in the
          City of Death.
If you make love with the divine now, in the next life
you will have the face of satisfied desire.

Kabir says this: When the Guest is being searched for,
it is the intensity of the longing for the Guest that
does all the work.

Kabir

A Note on the Texts and Calligraphy

Most of the selections chosen for this book were written over a span of more that thirteen hundred years. They were originally written in Arabic, Persian, Turkish, Hindi, Urdu, French, and other languages as well as in English. The translations tended to be uneven: some were heart-openingly beautiful; others were stuffy, archaic, pseudobiblical, or just confusing. We have revised the translations only as necessary to bring them closer to their dazzling originals. We are not the first to try to overcome the distance between vastly different languages. Edward FitzGerald published a number of versions of Omar Khayyám's *Rubaiyat,* and Coleman Barks's poetic genius has given us interpretative translations of many of Rumi's poems.

William Chittick and Peter Wilson, the distinguished translators of the classic Sufi work *Divine Flashes,* by Fakhruddin 'Iraqi, describe their own work as we would describe ours: "We have tried to 'trans-create' as well as translate, to offer something that will stand on its own as a work in English literature and that will provide a more exact rendition of 'Iraqi's *meaning* than a merely literal translation could attain."

We have also included the works of several modern poets who have produced jewels inspired by Sufism. We are grateful that the stream of wisdom from the heart continues to flow and that the capacity that opens the heart is not limited to classical Sufi authors.

Poems from *The Essential Rumi,* translated by Coleman Barks (HarperSanFrancisco, 1995), are not included in this volume because that book serves as a companion to this one. We have, however, taken a number of selections from other collections of Rumi's work.

The original author of each passage has been identified as accurately as possible. However, some passages were handed to us by friends and teachers as unmarked gifts, and some represent the words of one teacher quoted by another, then used as an example by a third. In those cases the original author's name has been lost. If you wish to track down the source of a specific quotation, write to us and we will help you if we can.

All names have been spelled as simply as possible, with a minimum of accent marks.

The errors and omissions that remain are our own.

⤳

Islamic calligraphy is an ancient, well-developed art form. The major work of the Muslim calligrapher is the transcription of the Koran. For centuries, all Korans were handwritten by master calligraphers. It is a great responsibility to write a Koran manuscript, as the Koran is revered as a Divine revelation. Every word in it is the word of God; every letter is sacred. Because of this reverence for the Koran, calligraphers practice their craft for a lifetime, seeking to make each letter as perfect as possible.

Before beginning to write a Koran manuscript, the calligrapher recites a "Bismillah": "In the name of God, the Merciful, the Compassionate." Extremely devout individuals begin virtually every spiritual or religious action with this invocation. It is also the opening for every chapter of the Koran but one.

Most of the calligraphies found at the beginning of the chapters of this book are versions of the "Bismillah," executed in various styles and arrangements. The other calligraphies include "Muhammad" and *La ilahe ilallah,* "There are no gods; there is God."

Bibliography

Addas, C. *The Quest for Red Sulphur: The Life of Ibn 'Arabi.* Cambridge, England: Islamic Texts Society, 1993.

Angha, Nahid, translator. *Deliverance: Words from the Prophet Mohammad.* San Rafael, CA: International Association of Sufism Publications, 1995.

Arasteh, R. *Growth to Selfhood: The Sufi Contribution.* London: Routledge and Kegan Paul, 1980.

———. *Rumi, the Persian: Rebirth in Creativity and Love.* Tucson, AZ: Omen Press, 1972.

Attar, Fariduddin. *The Conference of the Birds.* Translated by C. S. Nott. 1916. Reprint, London: Routledge and Kegan Paul, 1961.

———. *Memoirs of the Saints.* Translated by Bankey Behari. Lahore, Pakistan: Sh. Muhammad Ashraf, 1965.

Badruddin, Sheikh. *Inspirations on the Path of Blame.* An interpretation and commentary by Sheikh Tosun Bayrak. Putney, VT: Threshold Books, 1993.

Bayat, M., and M. A. Jamnia. *Tales from the Land of the Sufis.* Boston: Shambhala Publications, 1994.

Burke, O. M. *Among the Dervishes.* New York: E. P. Dutton, 1975.

Chittick, W. C. *The Sufi Path of Knowledge.* Albany: State Univ. of New York Press, 1989.

———. *The Sufi Path of Love: The Spiritual Teachings of Rumi.* Albany: State Univ. of New York Press, 1983.

Elwell-Sutton, L. P. *Persian Proverbs.* London: John Murray, 1954.

Farzan, Massud. *The Tale of the Reed Pipe: Teaching of the Sufis.* New York: E. P. Dutton, 1974.

Feild, Reshad. *The Last Barrier: A Journey Through the World of Sufi Teaching.* New York: Harper and Row, 1976.

Friedlander, Shems. *When You Hear Hoofbeats, Think of a Zebra.* New York: Harper and Row, 1987.

al-Ghazzali. *The Alchemy of Happiness.* Translated by Claud Field. Lahore, Pakistan: Sh, Muhammad Ashraf, 1964.

———. *The Book of Knowledge.* Translated by Nabih Amin Faris. Lahore, Pakistan: Sh. Muhammad Ashraf, 1966.

———. *Ghazali's Book of Council for Kings.* Translated by F. R. C. Bagley. London: Oxford University Press, 1964.

———. *Invocations and Supplications.* Cambridge, England: Islamic Text Society, 1990.

———. *The Mysteries of Fasting.* Translated by N. A. Faris. Lahore, Pakistan: Muhammad Ashraf, 1968.

———. *On the Duties of Brotherhood.* Translated by Muhtar Holland. Woodstock, NY: Overlook Press, 1976.

———. *The Revival of Religious Sciences.* Translated by Bankey Behari. Farnham, Surrey, England: Sufi Publishing Company, 1972.

Ibn 'Arabi, M. *What the Seeker Needs.* Translated by T. Bayrak and R. Harris. Putney, VT: Threshold Books, 1992.

Ibn 'Ata' Illah. *The Book of Wisdom.* Translated by Victor Danner and Kwaja Abdullah Ansari. *Intimate Conversations.* Translated by Wheeler M. Thackston. New York: Paulist Press, 1975.

'Iraqi, Fakhruddin. *Divine Flashes.* Translated by William Chittick and Peter Wilson. New York: Paulist Press, 1982.

Jami. *Yusuf and Zulaikha: An Allegorical Romance.* Edited, abridged, and translated by David Pendlebury. London: Octagon Press, 1980.

al-Jilani, Abdul Qadir. *The Endowment of Divine Grace and the Spread of Divine Mercy.* Vol. 1. Philadelphia: Pearl Publishing House, 1990.

———. *The Secret of Secrets.* Interpreted by Shaykh Tosun Bayrak. Cambridge, England: Islamic Text Society, 1992.

Kabir. *The Bijak of Kabir.* Translated by Linda Hess and Shukdev Singh. San Francisco: North Point Press, 1983.

———. *The Kabir Book: Forty-four of the Ecstatic Poems of Kabir.* Versions by Robert Bly. Boston: Beacon Press, 1977.

Lewin, L. *The Diffusion of Sufi Ideas in the West.* Boulder, CO: Keysign Press, 1972.

Lewis, Samuel L. *In the Garden.* New York: Harmony Books, 1975.

Moinuddin, Hakim. *The Book of Sufi Healing.* New York: Inner Traditions International, 1985.

Nasreddin, Hodja. *202 Jokes of Nasreddin Hodja.* Istanbul: Minyatür Yayinlari, n.d.

Nicholson, Reynold A. *The Mystics of Islam.* 1913. Reprint, London: Routledge and Kegan Paul, 1963.

Nurbakhsh, Javad. *The Great Satan, "Elbis."* London: Khaniqahi-Nimatullahi Publications, 1986.

―――. *Masters of the Path: A History of the Masters of the Nimatullahi Sufi Order.* London: Khaniqahi-Nimatullahi Publications, 1980.

―――. *The Psychology of Sufism.* London: Khaniqahi-Nimatullahi Publications, 1992.

―――. *Sufism.* Vol. 3. London: Khaniqahi-Nimatullahi Publications, 1985.

―――. *Traditions of the Prophet.* Vol. 1. London: Khaniqahi-Nimatullahi Publications, 1981.

Ozak, Muzaffer. *Irshad: Wisdom of a Sufi Master.* Amity, NY: Amity House, 1988.

―――. *Love Is the Wine: Talks of a Sufi Master in America.* Edited and compiled by Ragip Frager. Putney, VT: Threshold Books, 1987.

―――. *The Unveiling of Love.* New York: Inner Traditions International, 1981.

Ozelsel, M. *Forty Days: The Diary of a Traditional Solitary Sufi Retreat.* Putney, VT: Threshold Books, 1996.

Rumi, Jalal al-Din. *Crazy As We Are.* Translated by N. Ergin. Prescott, AZ: Hohm Press, 1992.

―――. *Discourses of Rumi.* Translated by A. J. Arberry. 1961. Reprint, New York: Samuel Weiser, 1972.

―――. *Like This: 43 Odes.* Versions by Coleman Barks. Athens, GA: Maypop Press, 1990.

―――. *Magnificent One.* Translated by N. Ergin. Burdett, NY: Larson Publications, 1993.

―――. *Rumi: Fragments, Ecstasies.* Translated by Daniel Liebert. Santa Fe: Source Books, 1981.

―――. *Say I Am You.* Translated by John Moyne and Coleman Barks. Athens, GA: Maypop Press, 1994.

Sa'di. *The Gulistan or Rose Garden.* Translated by Edward Rehatsek. New York: Capricorn Books, 1966.

al-Sadiq, Imam Ja'far. *The Lantern of the Path.* Shaftesbury, England: Element Books, 1989.

Sanai, Hakim. *The Walled Garden of Truth.* Translated and abridged by David Pendlebury. New York: E. P. Dutton, 1976.

Schimmel, A. *Mystical Dimensions of Islam.* Chapel Hill: Univ. of North Carolina Press, 1975.

Shafii, M. *Freedom from the Self: Sufism, Meditation and Psychotherapy.* New York: Human Sciences Press, 1985.

Shah, Idries. *Seeker After Truth.* London: Octagon Press, 1982.

———. *Tales of the Dervishes.* New York: E. P. Dutton, 1970.

———. *The Way of the Sufi.* New York: E. P. Dutton, 1970.

Smith, Margaret. *Rabia, the Mystic, A.D. 717–801, and Her Fellow Saints in Islam.* 1928. Reprint, San Francisco: Rainbow Bridge, 1977.

———. *Readings from the Mystics of Islam.* London: Luzac and Company, 1972; Westport, CT: Pir Press, 1994.

Suhrawardi, Shihabuddin Yahya. *The Mystical and Visionary Treatises.* Translated by W. M. Thackston, Jr. London: Octagon Press, 1982.

al-Suhrawardi, Abū al-Najib. *A Sufi Rule for Novices.* Abridged and translated by Menahem Milson. Cambridge: Harvard University Press, 1975.

Swami, Ghanananda, and John Stewart-Wallace. *Women Saints East and West.* Hollywood, CA: Vedanta Press, 1979.

Türkmen, Erkan. *The Essence of Rumi's Masnevi.* Misket, Konya, Turkey, 1992.

Tweedie, Irina. *The Chasm of Fire.* Tisbury, Wiltshire, England: Element Books, 1979.

Vaughan-Lee, L. *Travelling the Path of Love.* Inverness, CA: Golden Sufi Center, 1995.

Vitray-Meyerovitch, Eva de. *Rumi and Sufism.* Translated by Simone Fattal. Sausalito, CA: Post-Apollo Press, 1987.

Permission Acknowledgments

We are grateful to the following for permission to include excerpts from previously published works as well as original material:

Coleman Barks for permission to quote a selection from *Rumi: Like This: 43 Odes* (Athens, GA: Maypop Press, 1990) and a translation of a story by Bawa Muhaiyaddeen, © Bawa Muhaiyaddeen Fellowship.

Jeanette Berson, San Francisco Bay Area poet and artist, for permission to print one poem and one story.

Robert Bly for permission to quote from *The Kabir Book: Forty-four of the Ecstatic Poems of Kabir* (Boston: Beacon Press, 1977).

Dutton Signet for permission to reprint "A Talented Man Like You—An Example," "Joneyd and His Master," "Take My Hand," and "Attar and the Wandering Dervish" from *The Tale of the Reed Pipe* by Massud Farzan. Copyright © 1974 by Massud Farzan. Used by permission of Dutton Signet, a division of Penguin Books USA Inc.

John Murray Ltd. for permission to quote from *Persian Proverbs* by E. P. Elwell-Sutton.

John Fox, author of *Finding What You Didn't Lose: Expressing Your Truth and Creativity Through Poem-Making* (Tarcher/Putnam, 1995) and *Poetic Medicine: The Healing Art of Poetry-Making* (Tarcher/Putnam, 1997), for permission to quote a poem from *When Jewels Sing* (1989), Open Heart Publishers, P.O. Box 60189, Palo Alto, CA 94306.

of St. Paul the Apostle in the State of New York. Used by permission of Paulist Press.

Pir Publications for permission to quote from *Irshad: Wisdom of a Sufi Master* by Sheikh Muzaffer Ozak al-Jerrahi.

Selections from *Tales from the Land of the Sufis* by Mojdeh Bayat and Mohamad Jamnia, © 1994. Reprinted by arrangement with Shambhala Publications, Inc. 300 Massachusetts Ave., Boston, MA 02115.

We have made our best efforts to locate all rights holders and request all necessary permissions. In the event of any errors or omissions, please bring them to our attention and accept our apologies. Any necessary changes will be made in a subsequent printing.